Third International Workshop on NLP Solutions for Under Resourced Lanugages (NSURL 2022)

Online
18 December 2022

ISBN: 978-1-7138-9146-8

Printed from e-media with permission by:

Curran Associates, Inc.
57 Morehouse Lane
Red Hook, NY 12571

CURRAN ASSOCIATES INC. proceedings.com

Some format issues inherent in the e-media version may also appear in this print version.

Printed with permission by Curran Associates, Inc. (2024)

Association for Computational Linguistics
209 N. Eighth Street
Stroudsburg, Pennsylvania 18360

Phone: 1-570-476-8006
Fax: 1-570-476-0860

acl@aclweb.org

Additional copies of this publication are available from:

Curran Associates, Inc.
57 Morehouse Lane
Red Hook, NY 12571 USA
Phone: 845-758-0400
Fax: 845-758-2633
Email: curran@proceedings.com
Web: www.proceedings.com

NSURL 2022

Proceedings of the third International Workshop on NLP Solutions for Under Resourced Languages (NSURL 2022) co-located with ICNLSP 2022

December 18, 2022 (virtual)

DataScientia
Unitas per Varietatem

KNOW
DIVE

Tshwane University
of Technology

We empower people

SIG-UL

http://nsurl.org/

Introduction

Welcome to NSURL2022, the third International Workshop on NLP Solutions for Under Resourced Languages, held online on December 18th 2022, co-located with ICNLSP 2022.
NSURL is a forum for researchers and students to exchange ideas and discuss research and trends in the field of Natural Language Processing and Speech Processing for under resourced languages.
Fourteen papers have been submitted to NSURL 2022. Seven of them have been accepted. All the papers have been presented orally.
We would like to acknowledge the support provided by University of Trento and Data-Scientia. We would like also to express our gratitude to the organizing and the program committees for the hard and valuable contributions.

Abed Alhakim Freihat and Mourad Abbas

Organizers:

Chair: Dr. Abed Alhakim Freihat
Co-chair: Dr. Mourad Abbas

Program Committee:

Abed Alhakim Freihat, University of Trento **(Chair)**
Mourad Abbas, HCLA, Algeria
Ahmed AbuRa'ed, Universitat P. F. Barcelona, Spain
Abdallah Abushmaes, Mawdoo3 Ltd, Jordan
Abdulmohsen Althubaity, The National Center for Artificial Intelligence and Big Data (kacst), KSA
Sunday Ojo, Tshwane University of Technology Pretoria, South Africa
Violetta Cavalli-Sforza, Al Akhawayn University, Morocco
Heshaam Faili, University of Tehran, Iran
Mohammad Gharib, University of Florence, Italy
Osama Hamed, University of Duisburg-Essen, Germany
Linda van Huyssteen Tshwane University of Technology, Pretoria, South Africa
Hadi Khaliliya, Univeristy of Trento, Italy
Mohamed Lichouri, USTHB, Algeria
Nandu C Nair, Univeristy of Trento, Italy
Nasrin Taghizadeh, University of Tehran, Iran

Organizing Committee:

Hadi Khalilia, Univeristy of Trento
Nandu C Nair, Univeristy of Trento

Table of Contents

Syllable Subword Tokens for Open Vocabulary Speech Recognition in Malayalam. 1
Kavya Manohar, A. R. Jayan and Rajeev Rajan

Semi-Supervised and Unsupervised detection of Humour in Code-Mixed Hindi-English Tweets. 8
Chakita Muttaraju, Aakansha Singh, Anusha Kabber and Mamatha H. R.

Toward a Test Set of Dislocations in Persian for Neural Machine Translation. 14
Behnoosh Namdarzadeh, Nicolas Ballier, Lichao Zhu, Guillaume Wisniewski and Jean-Baptiste Yunès

Love Me, Love Me Not: Human-Directed Sentiment Analysis in Arabic. 22
Abraham Israeli, Aviv Naaman, Razan Assi, Yotam Nahum, Kfir Bar and Shai Fine

Eco EvE : Economic Event Extraction. 31
Meriem Mkhinini, Mohamed Ali Ben El Haj Aissa, Aboubacar Sidiki Sidibe, Paul Pike and Aymen Khelifi

An empirical Comparison of Arabic Named Entity Recognition Methods: Application to the ALP Corpus. . . 37
Mohamed Lichouri

ALRT: Cutting Edge Tool for Automatic Generation of Arabic Lexical Recognition Tests. 43
Osama Hamed, Saeed Salah and Abed Alhakim Freihat

Syllable Subword Tokens for Open Vocabulary Speech Recognition in Malayalam

Kavya Manohar* College of Engineering Trivandrum, India sakhi.kavya@gmail.com

A. R. Jayan Government Engineering College, Thrissur, India arjayan@gectcr.ac.in

Rajeev Rajan Government Engineering College, Trivandrum, India rajeev@cet.ac.in

Abstract

In a hybrid automatic speech recognition (ASR) system, a pronunciation lexicon (PL) and a language model (LM) are essential to correctly retrieve spoken word sequences. Being a morphologically complex language, the vocabulary of Malayalam is so huge and it is impossible to build a PL and an LM that cover all diverse word forms. Usage of subword tokens to build PL and LM, and combining them to form words after decoding, enables the recovery of many out of vocabulary words. In this work we investigate the impact of using syllables as subword tokens instead of words in Malayalam ASR, and evaluate the relative improvement in lexicon size, model memory requirement and word error rate.

1 Introduction

Malayalam belongs to the Dravidian family of languages with high morphological complexity (Manohar et al., 2020). Productive word formation in Malayalam by agglutination, inflection, and compounding leads to very long words with phonetic and orthographic changes at morpheme boundaries. This creates a large number of low frequency words and it is practically impossible to build a pronunciation lexicon that covers all complex wordforms.

A hybrid automatic speech recognition (ASR) decoder is built using an acoustic model, a language model (LM) and a pronunciation lexicon (PL). The acoustic model is a mapping between the acoustic features and the phonemes of the language (Georgescu et al., 2021). The LM is a learnt representation of word sequence probabilities. The PL is a dictionary where the pronunciation of each word or subword is described as a sequence of phonemes. These are composed into a weighted finite state transducer in a typical hybrid ASR decoder (Povey et al., 2011).

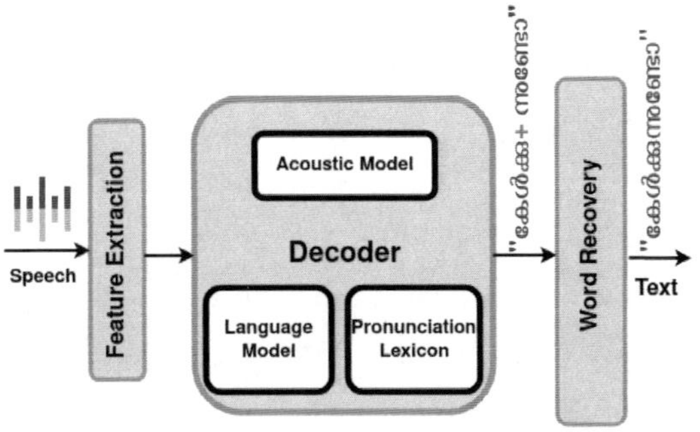

Figure 1: An open vocabulary hybrid ASR system, with subword based LM and PL.

Words not covered in the LM and the PL are called the out of vocabulary (OOV) words and they can not be recovered by the ASR decoder (Braun et al., 2021; Smit et al., 2021). However the use of subword tokens in an ASR for morphologically complex languages can recover a portion of OOV words by combining subword tokens to words. Figure 1 illustrates a hybrid open vocabulary ASR system. Special marker symbol '+' at subword boundaries enables the recovery of words.

Subword tokenization is carried out either through linguistically motivated rule based approaches or language independent data-driven approaches (Smit et al., 2021). However, there is no single algorithm that works fine for all languages. Even though the usage of subword tokenization for open vocabulary ASR has been thoroughly investigated (Hirsimäki et al., 2006; Choueiter et al., 2006; Wang et al., 2020; Zhou et al., 2021), there has not been much exploration in this regard in Malayalam language.

*Also affiliated with APJ Abdul Kalam Technological University, Kerala, India

Algorithm 1 Syllable Tokenization Algorithm

```
procedure SYLLABLE BOUNDARY TAGGING
    c_v ← consonant + virama
    Type 1 ← <BoW> + vowel+[anuswara, visarga, chillu] ?            ▷ ? indicates optionality
    Type 2 ← consonant + vowelsign ? + [anuswara, visarga, chillu]?
    Type 3 ← c_v * + consonant                                      ▷ * indicates one or more occurence
    Type 4 ← c_v ? + consonant + ◌ു? + virama + <EoW>
    syllable ← [Type 1, Type 2, Type 3, Type 4]                      ▷ Defines a syllable
    SyllableBoundaryTagger: <BoS>+ syllable + <EoS> ← syllable
end procedure
```

2 Related Works

Morpheme based subword tokenization has been proposed for ASR in many morphologically complex languages including Finnish, Arabic and Swedish (Choueiter et al., 2006; Smit et al., 2021). Syllable like units called vowel segments have been proposed to improve the ASR performance of Sanskrit, which is an inflectional language (Adiga et al., 2021). Data driven methods of tokenization using byte pair encoding (BPE) and Morfessor has been employed in the development of bilingual Hindi-Marathi ASR for improved performance and reduced complexity (Yadavalli et al., 2022). The sole work on the usage subword tokens for Malayalam ASR (Manghat et al., 2022) applies the linguistic information on a data-driven method to improve the word error rate (WER).

In the current work, we investigate the improvement that can be brought in by the linguistically motivated syllable subword tokens to address the issue of OOV recovery in Malayalam ASR. We evaluate the syllable subword ASR in terms of the WER, the lexicon size and the model memory requirement and compare it with the conventional word based PL and LM. This work is planned to be extended to analyse the impact of other data-driven methods for subword tokenization, in future.

3 Tokenization Algorithm

The characters in Malayalam script can be classified as: (i) vowels, (ii) vowel signs, (iii) consonants, (iv) special consonants (*anuswara*, *visarga* and *chillu*) and (v) the multi-functional character *virama*. A conjunct in Malayalam is a sequence of consonants separated by a *virama* in between. The writing system of Malayalam is alphasyllabary in nature (Bright, 1999). It means each standalone pronunciation unit is a syllable. If words are randomly split during tokenization, as in **SOPHIA** /soʊfiə/ being tokenized as **SOP** and **HIA**, the pronunciation can not be segmented in a valid way. Syllable tokens being valid pronunciation units, they can be described as a sequence of phonemes in the PL.

A syllable in Malayalam can be a consonant or a conjunct, followed by an optional vowel sign. A standalone vowel is also a syllable, that occur only at word beginnings. Whenever a special consonant appears, it becomes the syllable ending consonant (Nair, 2016). These linguistic rules for syllable tokenization has been computationally implemented as in Algorithm 1, by Manohar et al. (2022) and made available as part of the Mlphon Python library[1].

4 Datasets

We use the publicly available open licensed Malayalam read speech datasets in our experiments. Every speech recording is associated with a textual transcript in the Malayalam script. As shown in Table 1, we divide the available speech into train and test, ensuring that speakers and speech transcripts are not overlapped. The train datasets are combined to get 1125 minutes ($\approx$ 19 hours) of speech for acoustic model training. T1, T2 and T3 are the datasets used for testing. Except T3, all datasets are studio recorded read speech of formal sentences belonging to the same domain. T3 is mostly conversational sentences, recorded by volunteers in natural home environments, making it an out-of-domain test set.

To create the LM, we use the sentences from

[1] `https://pypi.org/project/mlphon/`

Table 1: Details of Speech datasets used in our experiments.

Name	Corpus	#Speakers	#Utterances	Duration (minutes)	Environment
Train 1	(Baby et al., 2016)	2	8601	838	Studio
Train 2	(He et al., 2020)	37	3346	287	Studio
T1	(Prahallad et al., 2012)	1	1000	98	Studio
T2	(He et al., 2020)	7	679	48	Studio
T3	(Computing, 2020b)	75	1541	98	Natural, Noisy

the speech transcripts and combine it with the curated collection of text corpus published by SMC (Computing, 2020a) that amounts to 205k unique sentences. From this, every sentence that appears in our test speech dataset is explicitly removed to prevent overfitting.

5 Methodology

To develop a hybrid ASR system, we need to build an acoustic model, an LM and a PL. The acoustic model is set as a common component in both word and syllable token based ASR. The LM is a statistical ngram model of words or syllables. To study the impacts of lexicon size we create word and syllable token based PL of different sizes. Each of these components is explained in the following subsections.

5.1 Acoustic Model

The acoustic model is trained using time delay neural networks (TDNNs) with Kaldi toolkit (Povey et al., 2011). Acoustic features used in TDNN training are: (i) 40-dimensional high-resolution MFCCs extracted from frames of 25 ms length and 10 ms shift and (ii) 100-dimensional i-vectors computed from chunks of 150 consecutive frames (Saon et al., 2013). Three consecutive MFCC vectors and the i-vector corresponding to a chunk are concatenated, resulting in a 220-dimensional feature vector for a frame (Georgescu et al., 2021). This acoustic model is trained on a single NVIDIA Tesla T4 GPU.

5.2 Language Models

A statistical view of how words are combined to form valid sentences is provided by the ngram model. Word sequence probabilities could be computed by analysing a large volume of text. In a 2-gram, a history of one previous word is required. We build ngram language models of orders n=2, 3 and 4 on the text corpus described in section 4 using SRILM toolkit (Stolcke, 2002).

Building LM using word tokens is straightforward, as *space* is considered as the default delimiter between words. However to build LM using syllable tokens instead of words, we need to syllabify the text corpus. Using Mlphon Python library, the text corpus is tokenized to syllables (Manohar et al., 2022). In order to identify syllables that occur at word medial positions, we have used '+' as a marker symbol.

Table 2: Samples of text from LM training corpus

Word	അവൻ വള ഇടുകയില്ല /aʋan ʋaɭa iʈukajilla/
Syllable	അ+ വൻ വ+ ള ഇ+ ടു+ ക+ യി+ ല്ല /a+ ʋan ʋa+ ɭa i+ ʈu+ ka+ ji+ lla/

In this approach, reconstruction of words is straightforward, as the marker indicates the positions for joining the following syllable. In the syllabified text, *space* is the delimiter between syllable tokens. Excerpts from the text copora used for training word and syllable token based LM are shown in Table 2.

5.3 Pronunciation Lexicons

Table 3: An excerpt from word PL and corresponding syllable PL.

Word PL		Syllable PL	
അവൻ	a ʋ a n	അ+	a
വള	ʋ a ɭ a	വൻ	ʋ a n
ഇടുകയില്ല	i ʈ u k a j i l l a	വ+	ʋ a
		ള	ɭ a
		ഇ+	i
		ടു+	ʈ u
		ക+	k a
		യി+	j i
		ല്ല	l l a

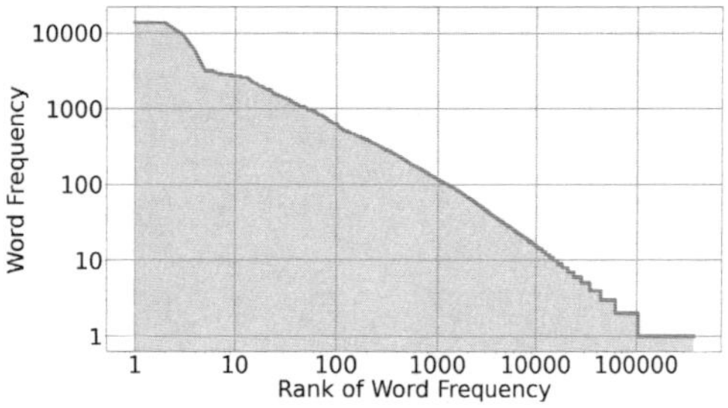

Figure 2: Logarithmic plot of word rank versus word frequency in the text corpus.

Sample entries in word PL and corresponding syllable PL are described in Table 3. To begin with, we create a word based PL that contains all unique words in the train audio transcripts which amounts to 25604 entries. This first lexicon is referred to as $PL1_W$. To study the impact of lexicon size on OOV rate and corresponding changes in WER, we expand $PL1_W$. New words are added to the lexicon based on their frequencies in the LM training corpus. When words in this corpus is ranked in the order of their frequencies, we obtain a word frequency profile as shown in Figure 2.

It can be seen that a huge portion of the corpus is covered by filling the PL with high frequency words. We add words with at least 5, 4, and 3 occurrences to $PL1_W$ to obtain the pronunciation lexicons $PL2_W$, $PL3_W$ and $PL4_W$ respectively. Subword lexicons PLi_S, with syllables as entries are derived from PLi_W, where $i = 1, 2, 3, 4$. The unique list of syllable tokens from every word PL is obtained to create the corresponding syllable PL. The number of entries in the syllable and word PL are presented in Table 4.

Table 4: The size of lexicons used in word and syllable based experiments

Lexicon	Size	Lexicon	Size
$PL1_W$	25604	$PL1_S$	3524
$PL2_W$	53240	$PL2_S$	5247
$PL3_W$	62483	$PL3_S$	5643
$PL4_W$	79950	$PL4_S$	6351

The syllable tokens corresponding to each word in PLi_W, is created with the marker symbol '+', as described in section 5.2. The pronunciation of word and syllable tokens in PLi_W and PLi_S are derived using Mlphon python library (Manohar et al., 2022).

6 Experimental Results

Combining the common acoustic model with the word LM, we build four different word based ASR by choosing one of PLi_W. Percentage of OOV words in different test datasets decreases with increase in the vocabulary size, as expected and is illustrated in Figure 3. Based on this, T1 can be considered as a low OOV test dataset, T2 a medium OOV test dataset and T3 a large OOV test dataset.

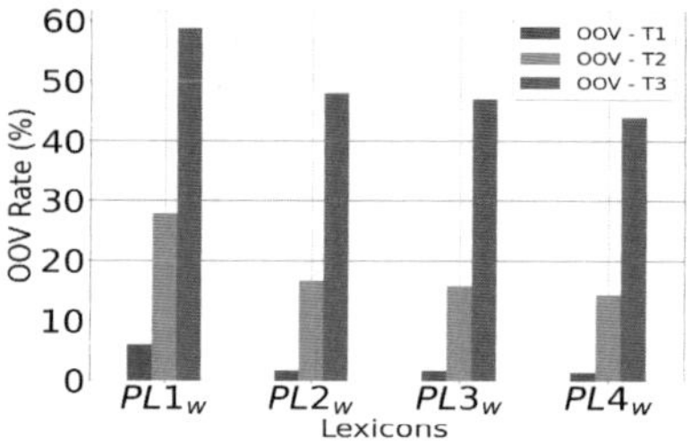

Figure 3: Lexicon size and OOV rate of test datasets

We repeat the above experiments with the LM training corpus and lexicons in syllabified form. Lexicons with syllables as entries are significantly smaller than word based lexicons, as indicated in Table 4 and are able to decode speech with improved WER on test datasets with medium to large OOV word rate. WER is computed by equation (1), based on the number of words inserted (I), deleted (D) and substituted (S) in the predicted speech when compared to the number of words (N) in ground truth transcript.

$$WER = \frac{I + D + S}{N} \quad (1)$$

We report the WER on different test datasets in Figure 4. On the test set T1, where OOV rates are very low (less than 6%), word based model perform well irrespective of ngram orders, the best being 9.8%, while the best WER given by syllable models on T1 is only 12%. It shows syllable tokens are not advantageous in terms of WER in low OOV scenarios. The WER is generally high as expected on the out of domain test set T3, where almost half the words are OOV and the recording environment is drastically different from the train datasets.

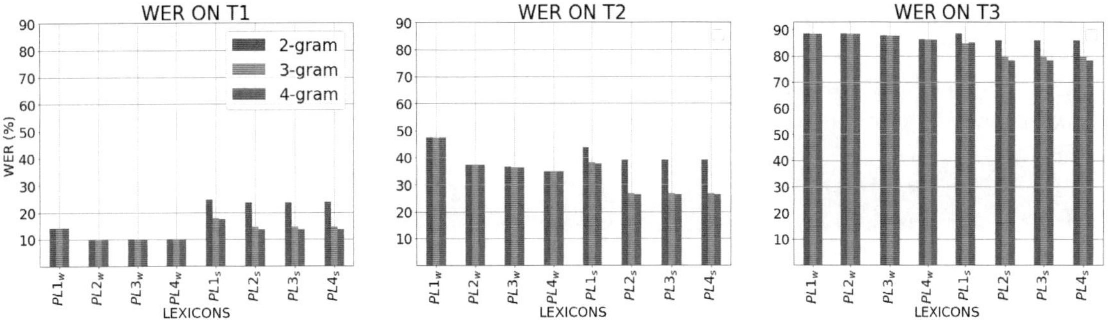

Figure 4: WER on different test datasets

Comparing the best WER, syllable based lexicons shows an improvement by 10% on T2 and by 7% on T3 than the corresponding word models. Since the previously published work on subword ASR for Malayalam (Manghat et al., 2022), was tested on a private dataset, the comparison of results is not meaningful and hence not attempted.

Ngram order and WER

For the word PL, increasing the ngram order imparts only nominal improvement in WER. This could be attributed to the sparse distribution of words due to the morphological complexity of Malayalam. The WER of the syllable PL does not show an improvement than the word PL for ngram order of 2. But the WER on syllable PL drastically reduces by 12% on T2 and by 6% on T3, when ngram order is increased from 2 to 3 and then it stabilizes. The mean word length in our test datasets is 3.2 syllables, providing the cause for the greatest improvement at this ngram transition.

Ngram order and Model Size

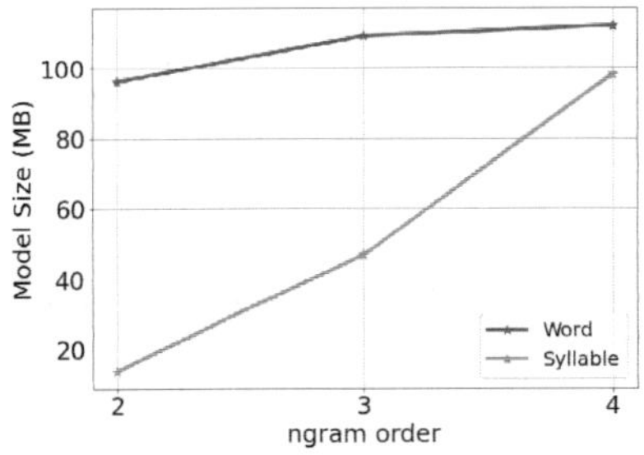

Figure 5: Model Size for word and syllable ASR.

To study the the model memory requirement, we compute the size of weighted FST graph (*HCLG.fst*) used for decoding. The model sizes corresponding to the largest word and syllable lexicons $PL4_W$ and $PL4_S$, where the WER are the best, are presented in Figure 5.

The memory requirement is generally high for word based models and it increases with the ngram order. The syllable tokens with much lower memory requirement at smaller ngram orders, show a rapid rise in model size with the increase in ngram order. There is a trade-off between the model size and the WER, while choosing the ngram order. For the ngram order of 3, ASR with syllable tokens having half the model size perform better in WER by 6% than the best word based model, as illustrated in Figures 4 and 5.

Lexicon Size and WER

There is a substantial WER improvement, when switching from $PL1_W$ to $PL2_W$ and $PL1_S$ to $PL2_S$, where the reduction in OOVs is the largest. Improvement in WER with subsequent lexicon expansions is nominal, as the added entries in the lexicons are low frequency words.

7 Conclusions

The comprehensive evaluation of syllables as subword tokens for building an open vocabulary hybrid ASR model is a pioneer attempt of its kind in Malayalam language. The proposed syllable based LM and PL in Malayalam demonstrate remarkable improvement in WER on medium and large OOV test sets, by 10% and 7% respectively . If the test datasets are free from OOV words, word based models outperform syllable models. Furthermore, syllable models with about half the model size have better WER than the corresponding word based ones, proving the effectiveness of syllable token based subword modelling on morphologically complex language like Malayalam. The optimal choice of ngram order based on the trade-off between model size and WER, depends on the subword tokenization technique. This study opens scope for investigating the impacts of other subword tokenization methods for Malayalam ASR.

References

Devaraja Adiga, Rishabh Kumar, Amrith Krishna, Preethi Jyothi, Ganesh Ramakrishnan, and Pawan Goyal. 2021. Automatic speech recognition in Sanskrit: A new speech corpus and modelling insights. In *Findings of the Association for Computational Linguistics: ACL-IJCNLP 2021*, pages 5039–5050. Association for Computational Linguistics.

Arun Baby, Anju Leela Thomas, NL Nishanthi, TTS Consortium, et al. 2016. Resources for Indian languages. In *Proceedings of Text, Speech and Dialogue*. CBBLR Workshop.

Rudolf A. Braun, Srikanth Madikeri, and Petr Motlicek. 2021. A Comparison of Methods for OOV-Word Recognition on a New Public Dataset. In *ICASSP 2021 - 2021 IEEE International Conference on Acoustics, Speech and Signal Processing (ICASSP)*, pages 5979–5983.

William Bright. 1999. A Matter of Typology: Alphasyllabaries and Abugidas. *Written Language & Literacy*, 2(1):45–55.

G. Choueiter, D. Povey, S.F. Chen, and G. Zweig. 2006. Morpheme-Based Language Modeling for Arabic LVCSR. In *2006 IEEE International Conference on Acoustics Speech and Signal Processing Proceedings*, volume 1, pages I–I.

Swathanthra Malayalam Computing. 2020a. Malayalam text corpora. In *Gitlab Repository*.

Swathanthra Malayalam Computing. 2020b. Releasing Malayalam speech corpus. In *SMC Website*.

Alexandru-Lucian Georgescu, Alessandro Pappalardo, Horia Cucu, and Michaela Blott. 2021. Performance vs. Hardware Requirements in state-of-the-art Automatic Speech Recognition. *EURASIP Journal on Audio, Speech, and Music Processing*, 2021(1):1–30.

Fei He, Shan-Hui Cathy Chu, Oddur Kjartansson, Clara Rivera, Anna Katanova, Alexander Gutkin, Isin Demirsahin, Cibu Johny, Martin Jansche, Supheakmungkol Sarin, and Knot Pipatsrisawat. 2020. Open-source Multi-speaker Speech Corpora for Building Gujarati, Kannada, Malayalam, Marathi, Tamil and Telugu Speech Synthesis Systems. In *Proceedings of The 12th Language Resources and Evaluation Conference (LREC)*, pages 6494–6503, Marseille, France. European Language Resources Association (ELRA).

Teemu Hirsimäki, Mathias Creutz, Vesa Siivola, Mikko Kurimo, Sami Virpioja, and Janne Pylkkönen. 2006. Unlimited Vocabulary speech recognition with Morph Language Models applied to Finnish. *Computer Speech & Language*, 20(4):515–541.

Sreeja Manghat, Sreeram Manghat, and Tanja Schultz. 2022. Hybrid Sub-word Segmentation for Handling Long Tail in Morphologically Rich Low Resource Languages. In *ICASSP 2022*, pages 6122–6126.

Kavya Manohar, A. R. Jayan, and Rajeev Rajan. 2020. Quantitative Analysis of the Morphological Complexity of Malayalam Language. In *International Conference on Text, Speech, and Dialogue*, pages 71–78. Springer.

Kavya Manohar, A. R. Jayan, and Rajeev Rajan. 2022. Mlphon: A Multifunctional Grapheme-Phoneme Conversion Tool Using Finite State Transducers. *IEEE Access*, 10:97555–97575.

V. R. Prabodhachandran Nair. 2016. *Introduction to Linguistics (ഭാഷാശാസ്ത്രപരിചയം /bʱaːʂaːʃaːst̪raparit͡ʃajam/)*. MaluBen Publications, Thiruvananthapuram, Kerala.

Daniel Povey, Arnab Ghoshal, Gilles Boulianne, Lukas Burget, Ondrej Glembek, Nagendra Goel, Mirko Hannemann, Petr Motlicek, Yanmin Qian, Petr Schwarz, et al. 2011. The Kaldi speech recognition toolkit. In *IEEE 2011 workshop on automatic speech recognition and understanding*, CONF. IEEE Signal Processing Society.

Kishore Prahallad, E. Naresh Kumar, Venkatesh Keri, S Rajendran, and Alan W Black. 2012. The IIIT-H Indic speech databases. In *Thirteenth annual conference of the international speech communication association*.

George Saon, Hagen Soltau, David Nahamoo, and Michael Picheny. 2013. Speaker adaptation of neural network acoustic models using i-vectors. In *2013 IEEE Workshop on Automatic Speech Recognition and Understanding*, pages 55–59. IEEE.

Peter Smit, Sami Virpioja, and Mikko Kurimo. 2021. Advances in subword-based HMM-DNN speech recognition across languages. *Computer Speech & Language*, 66:101158.

Andreas Stolcke. 2002. SRILM-an extensible language modeling toolkit. In *Seventh international conference on spoken language processing*.

Weiran Wang, Guangsen Wang, Aadyot Bhatnagar, Yingbo Zhou, Caiming Xiong, and Richard Socher. 2020. An Investigation of Phone-Based Subword Units for End-to-End Speech Recognition. In *Proc. Interspeech 2020*, pages 1778–1782.

Aditya Yadavalli, Shelly Jain, Ganesh Mirishkar, and Anil Kumar Vuppala. 2022. Investigation of subword-based bilingual automatic speech recognition for indian languages. In *Proceedings of the 2022 Fourteenth International Conference on Contemporary Computing*, IC3-2022, page 234–241, New York, NY, USA. Association for Computing Machinery.

Wei Zhou, Mohammad Zeineldeen, Zuoyun Zheng, Ralf Schlüter, and Hermann Ney. 2021. Acoustic Data-Driven Subword Modeling for End-to-End Speech Recognition. In *Proc. Interspeech 2021*, pages 2886–2890.

Semi-Supervised and Unsupervised detection of Humour in Code-Mixed Hindi-English Tweets

Chakita Muttaraju, Aakansha Singh, Anusha Kabber, Mamatha H R
Dept. of CSE.
PES University
Bangalore, India
{chakitapesu, sudhasingh538, anushakabber}@gmail.com,mamathahr@pes.edu

Abstract

A significant portion of social media consists of code-mixed data, as the number of users from India continues to grow rapidly. The phenomenon of mixing words belonging to different languages in conversations is referred to as code-mixing. As we continue to advance our social networks, it becomes imperative to accurately classify posts so they may be seen by a wider, more appropriate audience. Classification becomes harder in light of a substantial lack of labeled Hindi-English ground-truth data - owing to the inconvenience of human annotation and the relative difficulty of scraping. Supervised methods tend to suffer from such a deficiency of labeled data, especially SOTA models which require a considerable number of labeled examples to give good results. Hence, this paper outlines a novel semi-supervised method that can be used for binary classification of humorous Hindi-English code-mixed data. The GAN-BERT architecture (Croce et al., 2020) is modified to optimize results for code-mixed data. The paper also contrasts this method with various unsupervised techniques. We look into different embedding techniques such as LASER, FastText, and BERT for unsupervised classification. Fine-tuned Hinglish BERT integrated into the GAN-BERT architecture surpassed all other methods on the test set with an accuracy of 87.5%.

1 Introduction

In a multilingual society, the usage of code-mixed languages is a common occurrence. A significant part of the content available on social media is code mixed. This code-mixed data is a challenge in the field of natural language processing because its characteristics completely vary from the traditional structures of standard languages. This makes the processing of such content significantly harder. Humor Detection has been one of the most intriguing problems in Natural Language Processing as it requires a deep semantic understanding of the text. Most past research has been focused on detecting humor in unmixed languages but owing to the tremendous amount of code-mixed data available online there is a need to develop ways to detect humor in code- mixed data as well. We are also aware that obtaining labeled data for any task is a costly and time-consuming process. A viable solution to this problem is adopting a semi-supervised approach to identify the patterns even in a small dataset. One such semi-supervised method is implemented within the Semi-Supervised Generative Adversarial Network BERT (SS-GAN-BERT) .(Croce et al., 2020) The model takes a combination of labeled and unlabelled data as input where the proportion of labeled data is significantly smaller than the unlabelled samples. Here, a generator produces "fake" examples resembling the data distribution, while BERT is used as a discriminator.

In this work, we explore semi-supervised and unsupervised approaches for detecting humor in code-mixed languages. The semi-supervised method deals with modifying the current GAN-BERT architecture by replacing the BERT model with multiple specialized, regional language-based BERT models. This also adds a novel aspect to our study since this kind of approach has not been used before to the best of our knowledge. Additionally, for the semi-supervised methods, this paper also experiments with semi-supervised SGD. Unsupervised methods include obtaining sentence embeddings of Hindi-English code mixed data and clustering to classify them into humorous and non-humorous sections.

2 Related Work

Many researchers and practitioners from industry and academia have been attracted to the problem of text classification of code-mixed languages and humor detection. (Arora, 2020)proposed pretraining ULMFiT on synthetically generated code-mixed data, generated by modeling code-mixed data generation as a Markov process using Markov chains. (Gautam et al., 2021) used pre-trained models, fine-tuned on English-only tasks, and fine-tuned these models on translated code mixed datasets and achieved state-of-the-art results. To translate English-Hindi code mixed data to English, mBART was used. Here, words were transliterated informally without any standard rules and no formal data sources were used. (Yadav and Chakraborty, 2020) provides an experimental analysis of logistic regression, naive Bayes, decision tree, random forest, and SVM on our code-mixed data for classification tasks so as to create a benchmark for further research. They have also created a corpus for Dravidian languages in the context of sentiment analysis and offensive language detection tasks. (Conneau et al., 2019) has shown that cross-lingual embeddings can be made in a totally unsupervised way, i.e. they only require monolingual embeddings of the respective languages

3 Dataset

This dataset is populated with Hindi-English code mixed tweets scraped from Twitter. It is a subset of the dataset mentioned in the paper (Khandelwal et al., 2018). The creators of the original dataset used Python's twitterscraper to build the corpus. The tweets were annotated manually. Facts were automatically considered non-humorous and insults, irony, jokes, and anecdotes were labeled as humorous. An agreement of 0.821 Fleiss' and Kappa score for inter-annotator measure was achieved while annotating this dataset. The makers made sure to keep a good mix of topics in the dataset as they did not want the tweets to be domain dependent and the classification to be based upon semantic differences.

The original dataset, as available today, has a collection of tweet IDs without the tweet text. A number of tweets from this dataset have been removed from the platform. With the use of Twitter API v2, we were able to retrieve the text of the remaining tweets for training.

For the semi-supervised approach, the data was divided into a ratio of 1:100 for labeled vs unlabelled tweets as suggested by the authors of the original GAN-BERT paper(Croce et al., 2020). We used 46 labeled tweets and 4616 unlabelled tweets from the dataset. For testing, we used another 296 tweets. We attempted to keep an even distribution of humorous vs non-humorous tweets in each of the three sections: labeled, unlabelled, and test data. For unlabelled tweet data, the labels of tweets available in the corpus were removed and replaced with a placeholder 'UNK'. For the unsupervised approach, all 4662 tweets were stripped of their labels and clustered. Once more, 296 tweets were used as the test set.

4 Proposed Method

We are well aware that code mixed languages are under-resourced and obtaining annotated data for them is a costly process. In this work, we explore techniques that rely more on unlabeled data, which is easier to procure, and hence we utilize various semi-supervised and unsupervised models for the task of humor detection in code-mixed tweets. For semi-supervised models, we ran experiments by varying the BERT models, epochs, and dropout rate whereas for unsupervised models we try combinations for different word embeddings with various clustering algorithms. '

4.1 Semi-Supervised Method

We utilize the GAN-BERT architecture (Croce et al., 2020). As specified in their paper, we use a ratio of 1:100 as the ratio between labeled and unlabelled examples. The Generator component generates a set of fake samples from a given noisy distribution. The unlabelled and labeled samples are vectorized using the BERT model. The fake samples along with vectors for the unlabelled and labeled samples are fed in as input to the discriminator component which then learns to classify the data as fake or as belonging to one of the labels. As in SS-GANs(Khanuja et al., 2021), the labeled material is initially used to train the discriminator, i.e., the BERT model, and it is trained to differentiate between generated and real samples. Additionally, the discriminator is used to label or classify the real samples. In our case, these classes would be humorous vs. non-humorous. For the purpose of this work, we substitute the standard BERT model (Devlin et al., 2018) with multilingual BERT models such as IndicBERT (Kakwani et al., 2020) and MuRIL (Khanuja et al., 2021). Additionally, we use BERT models pre-trained and fine-tuned on Hinglish data such as HinglishBERT (verloop, 2021)(ketan rmcf, 2021) and HingBERT (l3cube pune, 2021). We trained the modified GAN-BERT on a code-mixed dataset with a number of different optimizations to improve performance, including testing multiple different BERT models to replace the original BERT in the GAN-BERT architecture. Number of epochs, batch size, and dropout rate were also experimented with to achieve the best performance.

IndicBERT IndicBERT is a version of ALBERT (Lan et al., 2019) for Indian languages. It is a multilingual language model trained on a huge corpus of some of the most popular Indian languages - Hindi, Kannada, Bangali, Tamil, Telugu, and many more. IndicBERT is said to give state-of-the-art performances for multiple language tasks in regional languages. It also uses much fewer parameters compared to models like XLM-R and mBERT. We use IndicBERT under the assumption that IndicBERT will perform better than BERT in the case of code-mixed Hindi-English data, the latter having been purely trained in English.

We found that IndicBERT does perform better than BERT with an approximate accuracy improvement of 10%. While this is true, for our specific dataset, IndicBERT does not outperform every other model chosen in this paper. This can be attributed to the fact that IndicBERT was trained on large corpora of Indian languages in their original scripts and none of the data was code-mixed. These corpora were not transliterated.

We have also seen IndicBERT achieve the highest accuracy at around 10 training epochs and a dropout rate of 0.2.

MuRIL MuRIL was assumed to be an improvement from the IndicBERT model as it is trained on transliterated Indian languages. MuRIL is a BERT model that is trained on 17 different Indian languages and their transliterated counterparts. The model is trained similarly to multilingual BERT only that it uses an exponent value of 0.3 and not 0.7 for upsampling which is shown to enhance low-resource performance.

It was observed that MuRIL did marginally better than IndicBERT at its highest point. An interesting factor for MuRIL was that the accuracy did not drop as the number of epochs increased and it maintained a respectable, fairly high accuracy when quite a few of the other models started to overfit and perform worse.

HinglishBERT These models are BERT models specifically trained on Hindi-English code-mixed data. Furthermore, this data was also scraped from code-mixed data from Twitter. The authors train and then fine-tune these models on hundreds of thousands of code-mixed tweets from a Twitter stream.

The fine-tuned HinglishBERT was by far our best model for classifying tweets when trained in a generative adversarial setting. It outperformed our second-best model by approximately 7%. We also observed that this model starts to overfit and perform worse after training for around 25 epochs or more. We attribute it to the dataset HinglishBERT was trained on. This also reinforces the authors' statement that declares fine-tuning on code-mixed data improves the model's performance as HinglishBERT did not perform quite as well as fine-tuned HinglishBERT did by quite a large margin.

HingBERT HingBERT is a BERT model that is pre-trained on a corpus that is the first of its kind with 52.93M Hindi-English code-mixed sentences. As expected, HingBERT performed similarly to HinglishBERT and better than IndicBERT with a lot of similar data sources compared to our dataset.

4.1.1 Semi-supervised SGD

In this work, we have explored another semi-supervised classification technique implemented by the self-training algorithm. In this method, we first train a classifier on the available labeled observations. After this, we use the obtained classifier to predict the classes of unlabeled samples. From these, we pick the observations that satisfy particular criteria like prediction probability and use these as 'pseudo-labels' along with the labeled data for training a new supervised model. We repeat the process for a certain number of iterations or till we run out of labeled data. We have used a Semi-supervised SGD classifier in combination with different embeddings like TF-IDF and FastText. Of these embedding methods, TF-IDF gave the maximum accuracy of 78.5% whereas FastText gave 72.9%.

The results of the experiments are detailed in the Results section of this paper.

4.2 Unsupervised Method

This paper addresses the problem of the unavailability of labeled data by choosing to use semi-supervised and unsupervised methods. Sentence and word embeddings are commonly used to obtain clusters of different classes in unsupervised language classification tasks. Here, we converted our unlabeled dataset of 4600 tweets to sentence embeddings to then cluster them according to different clustering algorithms. We explore three different models that normally provide multilingual embeddings, but in this case are used to obtain embeddings for Hindi-English code-mixed data: 1) LASER, 2) FastText, 3) sentencetransformer-bert-hinglish.

LASER stands for Language-Agnostic Sentence Representations (Artetxe and Schwenk, 2019). As the name suggests these embeddings use a single model for a variety of languages. Since code-mixed languages come under the category of the so-called low resource languages, LASER embeddings can be used for obtaining a vector representation for them.

FastText is a subword level embedding based on the skipgram model of word2vec (Bojanowski et al., 2016). Since code-mixed languages are riddled with spelling variations and inconsistencies and also there can code-mixing at the subword level, FastText seems to be a good choice for the sentiment analysis task.

The sentencetransformer-bert-hinglish generates a Transformer based representation for a low-resource language using existing representations in another high-resource language (Reimers and Gurevych, 2019).

We also compare the performance of different clustering algorithms, namely, K-Means clustering, Spectral Clustering, and Agglomerative Clustering for the sentiment analysis task.

5 Results

Multiple BERT models were used in the GAN-BERT architecture to construct semi-supervised methods. Additionally, semi-supervised SGD was also experimented with. Results from trials of unsupervised methods dealing with the clustering of sentence embeddings are also included. As expected, the semi-supervised methods performed better with Fine-tined HinglishBERT in the GAN-BERT architecture performing the best with 87.5% accuracy.

Semi-supervised methods performed better for a number of reasons - the models used to generate sentence embeddings were not specifically trained on Hindi-English code mixed data. Also, simple clustering based on humor, a fairly abstract concept, would not perform as well as the more customised, sophisticated semi-supervised methods used in this paper. Experiments based on unsupervised methods were still utilised for comparison to provide the reader an idea of how well the semi-supervised methods perform.

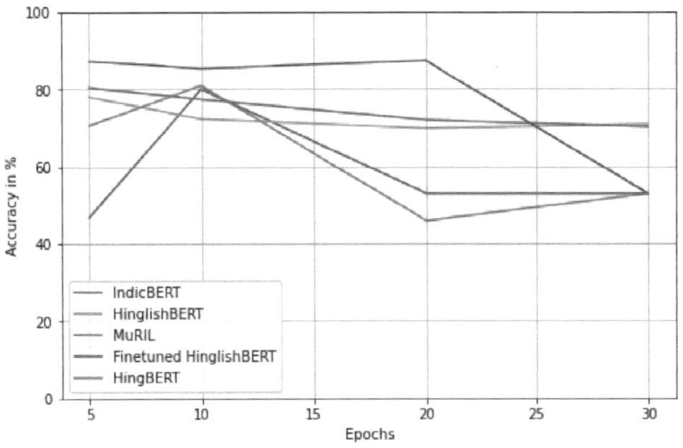

Figure 1: Accuracy improvement w.r.t increasing epochs.

5.1 Semi-supervised Methods

As mentioned before, we primarily ran experiments on the training of the GAN-BERT model on our dataset by the following processes: 1) Varying BERT models more suited to our specific language task., 2) Epochs, 3) Dropout rate.

Throughout these experiments, the training size was 4616 unlabeled tweets, and 46 labeled tweets and the test set was 296 tweets long.

The models were trained on a number of epochs and as seen in Figure 1, increasing the number of epochs did not improve performance in most cases. Fine-tuned HinglishBERT performed the best with an accuracy of 0.875 at 20 epochs.

In Table 1, models and their highest accuracy across epochs are given.

Table 1: Models and Accuracy

Model	Accuracy
BERT	0.689
Fine-tuned HinglishBERT	**0.875**
HinglishBERT	0.780
HingBERT	0.810
MuRIL	0.804
IndicBERT	0.800

We experimented with various dropout rates and found that these dropouts work best with the corresponding models as shown in Table 2.

Semi-supervised SGD resulted in an accuracy of 78.5% with TF-IDF as shown in Table 3.

Table 2: Models, Dropout Rate and Accuracy

Model	Dropout Rate	Accuracy
BERT	0.2	0.689
Fine-tuned HinglishBERT	**0.09**	**0.875**
HinglishBERT	0.7	0.780
HingBERT	0.1	0.810
MuRIL	0.09	0.804
IndicBERT	0.2	0.800

Table 3: Semi-supervised SGD and embeddings

Embedding	Accuracy
TF-IDF	**0.785**
FastText	0.729

5.2 Unsupervised Methods

For unsupervised methods, we obtained sentence embeddings from three different models: 1) LASER, 2) FastText, 3) sentencetransformer-bert-hinglish

and clustered these embeddings with three different clustering algorithms: 1) K-Means, 2) Spectral Clustering, and 3) Agglomerative Clustering.

The results of K-Means on the three different embeddings are shown in Figure 2.

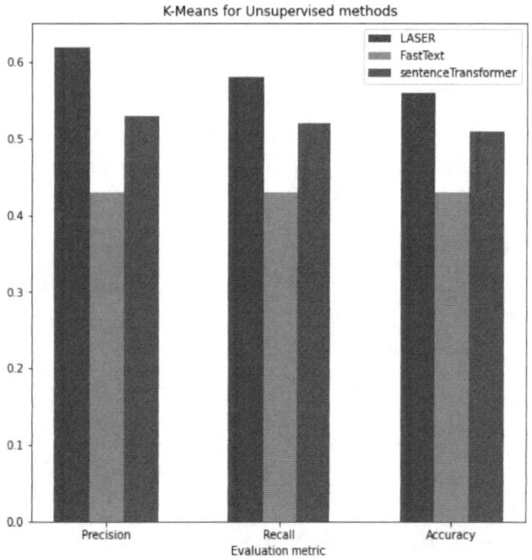

Figure 2: K-Means performed on the three different sentence embeddings obtained from three different models.

As can be observed, LASER had the highest average precision, recall, and accuracy when K-Means clustering was used. FastText easily performed the worst, getting accuracy scores of less than 0.5.

Spectral Clustering and its results are shown in Figure 3.

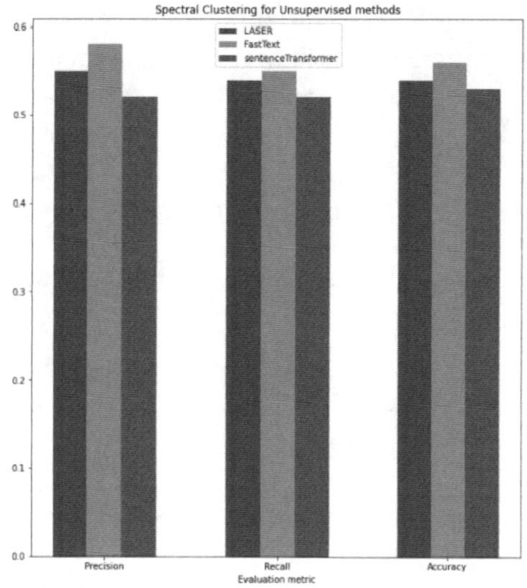

Figure 3: Spectral clustering performed on the three different sentence embeddings obtained from three different models.

With Spectral clustering, FastText had the upper hand but only slightly. The sentence transformer accuracy was barely above 0.5 for spectral clustering.

Agglomerative clustering showed a different story as shown in Figure 4.

LASER performed abysmally while sentence transformer and FastText stayed with a similar range of accuracy. No real improvement was shown.

Unsupervised methods, on a whole, did not achieve very high performance with the highest accuracy being LASER embeddings clustered with K-Means with an accuracy of 0.62.

Conclusion

We explored semi-supervised and unsupervised methods with the intent of classifying tweets as humorous or non-humorous. For semi-supervised methods, we chose to train different models in a generative adversarial setting similar to SS-GANs. We also experimented with a number of different parameters to get the highest accuracy possible. With unsupervised methods, we chose some of the most popular models to obtain multilingual sentence embeddings and clustered the embeddings with three different clustering algorithms. We found that semi-supervised methods outperform largely with Fine-tuned HinglishBERT leading the race with an accuracy of 0.875.

This research could be extended in a number of

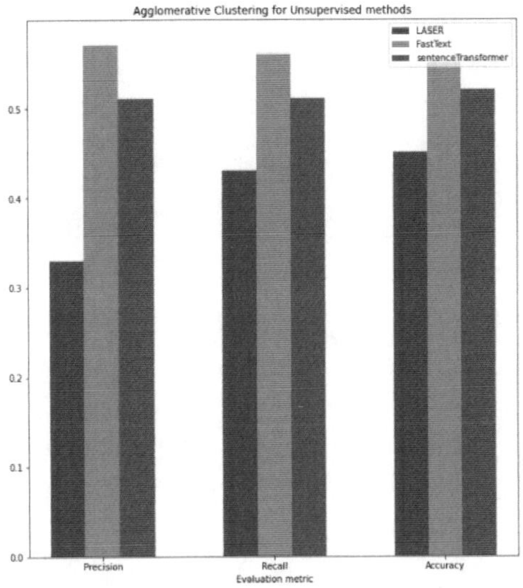

Figure 4: Agglomerative clustering performed on the three different sentence embeddings obtained from three different models.

ways. The length of the labeled and unlabeled sets is kept constant throughout the experiments. The number of labeled and unlabeled tweets could be increased to possibly achieve better accuracy. The ratio of the test set to train could be varied for a more rounded analysis.

References

Gaurav Arora. 2020. Gauravarora@ hasoc-dravidian-codemix-fire2020: pre-training ulmfit on synthetically generated code-mixed data for hate speech detection. *arXiv preprint arXiv:2010.02094*.

Mikel Artetxe and Holger Schwenk. 2019. Massively multilingual sentence embeddings for zero-shot cross-lingual transfer and beyond. *Transactions of the Association for Computational Linguistics*, 7:597–610.

Piotr Bojanowski, Edouard Grave, Armand Joulin, and Tomas Mikolov. 2016. Enriching word vectors with subword information.

Alexis Conneau, Kartikay Khandelwal, Naman Goyal, Vishrav Chaudhary, Guillaume Wenzek, Francisco Guzmán, Edouard Grave, Myle Ott, Luke Zettlemoyer, and Veselin Stoyanov. 2019. Unsupervised cross-lingual representation learning at scale. *arXiv preprint arXiv:1911.02116*.

Danilo Croce, Giuseppe Castellucci, and Roberto Basili. 2020. GAN-BERT: Generative adversarial learning for robust text classification with a bunch of labeled examples. In *Proceedings of the 58th Annual Meeting of the Association for Computational Linguistics*, pages 2114–2119, Online. Association for Computational Linguistics.

Jacob Devlin, Ming-Wei Chang, Kenton Lee, and Kristina Toutanova. 2018. Bert: Pre-training of deep bidirectional transformers for language understanding. *arXiv preprint arXiv:1810.04805*.

Devansh Gautam, Kshitij Gupta, and Manish Shrivastava. 2021. Translate and classify: Improving sequence level classification for english-hindi code-mixed data. In *Proceedings of the Fifth Workshop on Computational Approaches to Linguistic Code-Switching*, pages 15–25.

Divyanshu Kakwani, Anoop Kunchukuttan, Satish Golla, Gokul N.C., Avik Bhattacharyya, Mitesh M. Khapra, and Pratyush Kumar. 2020. IndicNLPSuite: Monolingual corpora, evaluation benchmarks and pre-trained multilingual language models for Indian languages. In *Findings of the Association for Computational Linguistics: EMNLP 2020*, pages 4948–4961, Online. Association for Computational Linguistics.

ketan rmcf. 2021. Fine-tuned HinglishBERT model on Huggingface.

Ankush Khandelwal, Sahil Swami, Syed S Akhtar, and Manish Shrivastava. 2018. Humor detection in english-hindi code-mixed social media content: Corpus and baseline system. *arXiv preprint arXiv:1806.05513*.

Simran Khanuja, Diksha Bansal, Sarvesh Mehtani, Savya Khosla, Atreyee Dey, Balaji Gopalan, Dilip Kumar Margam, Pooja Aggarwal, Rajiv Teja Nagipogu, Shachi Dave, Shruti Gupta, Subhash Chandra Bose Gali, Vish Subramanian, and Partha Talukdar. 2021. Muril: Multilingual representations for indian languages.

l3cube pune. 2021. HingBERT model on Huggingface.

Zhenzhong Lan, Mingda Chen, Sebastian Goodman, Kevin Gimpel, Piyush Sharma, and Radu Soricut. 2019. Albert: A lite bert for self-supervised learning of language representations. *arXiv preprint arXiv:1909.11942*.

Nils Reimers and Iryna Gurevych. 2019. Sentence-bert: Sentence embeddings using siamese bert-networks.

verloop. 2021. HinglishBERT model on Huggingface.

Siddharth Yadav and Tanmoy Chakraborty. 2020. Unsupervised sentiment analysis for code-mixed data. *arXiv preprint arXiv:2001.11384*.

Toward a Test Set of Dislocations in Persian for Neural Machine Translation

Behnoosh Namdarzadeh[1], Nicolas Ballier[1 2], Lichao Zhu[1], Guillaume Wisniewski[2], Jean-Baptiste Yunès[3]
[1]CLILLAC-ARP, [2]LLF, [3]IRIF
Université Paris Cité, F-75013 Paris, France
behnoosh.namdarzadeh@etu.u-paris.fr,
{nicolas.ballier, lichao.zhu, guillaume.wisniewski, jean-baptiste.yunes}@u-paris.fr

Abstract

This paper describes a test set designed to analyse the translation of dislocations from Persian, to be used for testing neural machine translation models. We first tested the accuracy of the two Universal dependency treebanks for Persian to automatically detect dislocations. Then we parsed the available Persian treebanks on GREW (Bonfante et al., 2018) to build a specific test set containing examples of dislocations. With available aligned data on OPUS (Tiedemann, 2016), we trained a model to translate from Persian into English on openNMT (Klein et al., 2017). We report the results of our translation test set by several toolkits (Google Translate, MBART-50 (Tang et al., 2020), Microsoft Bing and our in-house translation model) for the translation into English. We discuss why dislocations in Persian provide an interesting testbed for neural machine translation.

1 Introduction

This paper describes a first experiment (to the best of our knowledge) at building a neural machine translation test corpus relying on Persian dislocations. Dislocation is a structure that allows the repetition of a dislocated item with (usually) a proform that resumes the referent of the dislocated item like من، خودم... 'English: *I, myself ...*' 'French: *moi, je...*'. Previous research has shown that dislocations can be challenging for neural machine translation, because they tend to be very present in spoken data and consequently often under-represented in training data, resulting in mistranslations, for example from French into English where the dislocated item is often reduplicated with a second agrammatical subject (Namdarzadeh and Ballier, 2022). For neural machine translation (NMT), dislocations are therefore challenging and a perfect topic for a challenge set approach (Isabelle et al., 2017).

Persian still is as an under-resourced language for NLP tasks, as shown in the Proceedings of the NSURL Workshop (Freihat and Abbas, 2021). From a typological perspective, not only does Persian allow dislocation like many other languages, but also scrambling (?), so that investigating the translation of dislocated constructions raises interesting linguistic questions in the direction of fixed ordered languages like English. Our combination of languages is an interesting observatory to investigate the translation of word order. Two main research questions are addressed: do we observe an agrammatical copy of the dislocated item in the translation (syntactic adequacy) and is the information packaging effect of the dislocation rendered in the translation (pragmatic adequacy)?

The rest of the paper is structured as follows: Section 2 provides an overview of Machine Translation (MT) related resources for Persian. Section 3 explains how we collected the dislocations from existing Treebanks. Section 4 describes the translation model we produced. Section 5 analyses the translations produced by different MT systems we tested. Section 6 discusses our findings.

2 Previous Research and Resources

Persian, also known as Farsi, is an Indo-Iranian branch of the Indo-European family. Persian has three variants: Western Persian, referred to as 'Parsi' or 'Farsi' which is spoken in Iran. Eastern Persian referred to as 'Dari' and spoken in Afghanistan. And the last variant is Tajiki, which is spoken in Tajikistan and Uzbekistan

(Seraji, 2015).

2.1 Previous MT systems

One of the prototype translation systems that is able to translate Persian into English is the Shiraz machine translation project (Amtrup et al., 2000). Feeding the translation model with the higher size of parallel corpora from different domains improved the outputs of the system significantly (Mohaghegh, 2012). Years later, the emergence of MIZAN corpus, the biggest Persian-English parallel corpus, can be considered as an improvement in the field of machine translation. It consists of 1,021,596 Persian-English aligned sentences. An SMT system was developed using this corpus to observe the function of the translation model. Despite the acceptable BLEU score, the conclusion is that Persian remains an under-resourced language with comprehensive open issues (Kashefi, 2018).

2.2 Previous NMT systems

For neural machine translation (NMT), Persian is not (as yet?) implemented in DeepL but in Google Translate toolkit and no less than 14 APIs support Persian for MT [1]. Several dictionaries for English to Farsi are available online [2]. We resorted to the online versions of Google Translate, Bing Microsoft Translator (hereafter Bing) and MBART-50, the multilingual model developed for 50 languages (Tang et al., 2020).

2.3 Available UD Treebanks for Persian

For the analysis of Persian using Universal dependency (De Marneffe et al., 2006; De Marneffe and Manning, 2008), two treebanks have been developed: (Seraji et al., 2016) and (Rasooli et al., 2020) deriving from the Persian Dependency Treebank (Rasooli et al., 2013). We searched for examples of dislocations in the treebanks and report our findings in the following section.

3 Dislocations in Persian

3.1 Previous Research

Before beginning the typologies of plausible dislocated constructions in Persian, we have to pinpoint that Persian is a pro-drop language. This means that the agreement between the verb and its subject is realized by verbal suffixes (Faghiri and Samvelian, 2021); thus the subject can be dropped in a sentence. Persian displays free word order (Faghiri and Samvelian, 2021) but is an SOV language. There are some cases in Persian where the SOV canonical word ordering is changed based on the context. This can be clearly seen in a sentence where the constituent گل'flower' is positioned at the left side of the sentence, expressing the contrastive focus in the sentence گل علی برای مریم خرید 'flower Ali for Maryam buy-PST' that the subject buys گل 'flower' and not something else (Faghiri and Samvelian, 2021). The other dislocated element in Persian is quite similar to the French *ce que* structure. In the Persian sentence آنچه که گفت درست بود the sentence begins with آنچه (what), meaning *What (s)he said was right* (Faghiri and Samvelian, 2021). Furthermore, clefting is frequent in Persian, in a way that the focused element is moved to the initial position of a sentence. Various functions can be cloven except adverbs, like in the example توی باغ بود که همدیگر را دیدیم 'in garden be-PST that each other ra see-PL' the adjunct is cloven (Faghiri and Samvelian, 2021).

3.2 Data Collection with GREW

We also queried the UD_PersianSeraji treebank on the GREW project[3]. Figure 1 shows the "relation table" (Guibon et al., 2020) which displays the relations between a governor (here, selected with the category "dislocated") and the corresponding dependents, classified as columns according to their part of speech (here, nouns, pronouns and particles).

It can be also argued that manipulating some of the examples, placing the تو خودت in the left periphery of the sentence changes the detection of the constituent as `dislocated`. It seems that the number of words between the dislocated item and the constituent resumed by the constituent affects the detection of `dislocated`. Interestingly, in the examples taken from GREW, اینجا برنامه برای ارتباط با مخاطب خودش دچار مشکل می‌شود., there is a distance between the dislocated item برنامه and خودش, this is not recognized as a dislo-

[1] https://machinetranslate.org/persian

[2] e.g. https://translate.glosbe.com/en-fa/machine%20translation

[3] http://universal.grew.fr/?corpus=UD_Persian-Seraji@2.10

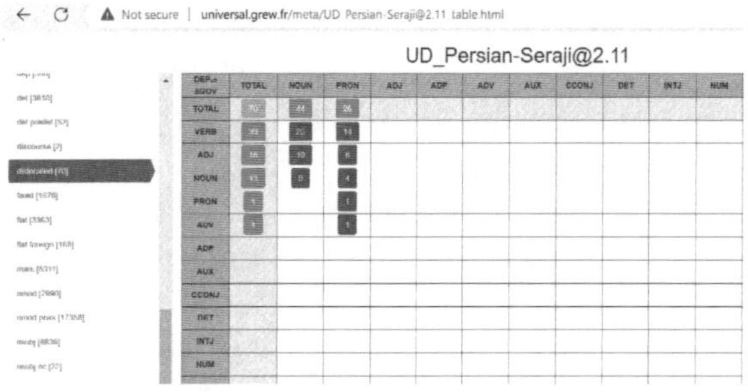

Figure 1: Distribution of Dependent items using GREW

cation item in UDPipe, whereas, in the می‌گویند چه جوری است که تهیه‌کننده خودش دارد تقلب می‌کند!, the dislocated item تهیه کننده and its resuming construction خودش is placed one after another with no distance. The {UDPipe} package (Wijffels, 2022) in R (R Core Team, 2022) can correctly detect it as a dislocated construction. Thus, it might be the case that the proximity of the proposed dislocated constituent to its referent could have an impact on their detection.

3.3 The Two UD Treebanks for Persian

Two Treebanks are currently available for Universal Dependency on github : Persian-Seraji and UD Persian. There are only two Treebanks available in the Universal Dependency (UD) framework. This can be a good reason to label Persian as an under-resourced language. One is PerUDT (Rasooli et al., 2013), which consists of 29,000 sentences extracted from contemporary Persian texts in different genres such as news, academic papers, articles and fictions. The other is UPDT Treebank (Seraji et al., 2016), which consists of 6,000 annotated and validated sentences of different genres. The `GREW-match` project also represents an analysis of the two above-mentioned treebanks in more details. It so happens that dislocations is a hapax in the reference Persian Dependency Treebank (Rasooli et al., 2013). The treebank contains 29,107 sentences and only one occurrence of 'dislocated' was spotted. For the purpose of this study, since no `dislocated` was found in PerUDT Treebank, we chose the UPDT Treebank. We review the dependency relations on `GREW-match` as well, to recheck the annotations and compile the Persian sentences with a `dislocated` dependency relation (deprel).

4 Material and Methods

This section describes how we built the neural translation engine we produced.

4.1 Tokenizations

We used BPE to tokenize English and Persian data sets into subwords by processing as follows: i) first word tokenization of datasets (train, dev, test) is applied with a standard tokenizer of each language; ii) training of a subword tokenization model with monolingual data; iii) a second subword tokenization is applied to the tokenized datasets; iv) training of our neural model with subword-tokenized English↔Persian parallel corpus.

To try to avoid subtokenisation issues, we trained our BPE model with a larger corpus. The data sets for the BPE model are split as follows: for English, we used `spaCy` (Honnibal and Johnson, 2015) library to tokenize a data set, by normalizing and compiling WMT15's Europarl, News Commentary and Common Crawl (Bojar et al., 2015) French↔English parallel corpus, which contains 116,035,319 words. The compiled data set was used to train a `SentencePiece` (Kudo, 2018) BPE model as follows : vocab-size=32000, character_coverage=1, model_type=unigram. As for Persian, we used `Stanza` (Qi et al., 2020) with the UD Persian Seraji Treebank (Qi et al., 2018) to tokenize a Farsi data set (98,472,761 words) from the CCAligned v1 corpus (El-Kishky et al., 2020), in order to train a `SentencePiece` BPE model with comparable data size and with the following parameters : vocab-size=32000, character_coverage=0.9995, model_type=unigram.

4.2 Training

We used TED2020 (Reimers and Gurevych, 2020) Farsi↔English parallel corpus (EN : 6,036,185 words, FA : 7,362,765 words) to train a neural machine translation model with `OpenNMT` (Klein et al., 2017). Both Farsi and English corpora are split into three data sets : `dev` (2,000 lines), `test` (2,000 lines) and `train` (the rest of the data set). `OpenNMT` implements a `transformer` model with the following architecture: 6 encoder and decoder layers; each layer has 8 attention heads; the feed-forward layers of the transformer have 2,046 parame-

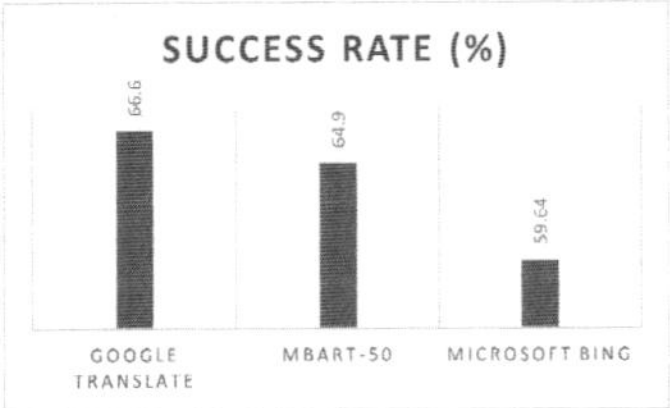

Figure 2: Success Rate of `dislocated` constituent translation

ters; the dimension of word embedding is 512. In the end, there are 72,924,862 parameters.

5 Results

5.1 Detection of Dislocation on Current UD Models

When parsing our test set with the {UDpipe}, only 17 cases out of 57 sentences were detected as dislocation. This means that only about 30% of our examples are recognized as a dislocated item in the test set. Interestingly, there seems to be an identifiable pattern through which dislocated dependency relations are identified. To give a concrete example, duplicated use of the subject is detected by {UDpipe} when singular (e.g. من for *I* or تو for *you*) but not so if plural. Yet, this is not even systematic.

5.2 Quality Evaluation of the Translations across NMT Toolkits

For the evaluation of the quality of the translations, we applied the "descriptive-comparative human analysis" model of Keshavarz , which suggests different types of errors in the outputs, to evaluate the translations (Zand Rahimi et al., 2017). What matters in our evaluation of the quality of the translations is the grammaticality of the translations. Our success rate is based on syntactic adequacy, i.e. avoiding copying the dislocated items in outputs. Compared with more elaborate criteria of human assessment methods (HA) which also analyse fluency and fidelity (Han et al., 2021), we mostly focused on (syntactic) adequacy and comprehension of the outputs rather than on subtle analyses of semantic and pragmatic adequacy. Figure 2 globally indicates success rates of the `dislocated` constituent translations across the different toolkits. Dislocation remains an issue for at least a third of our 57 examples. Among the three toolkits, Google Translate records the highest success rate (66.6 %), and Microsoft Bing gets the lowest rate (59.64%). MBART-50 is in between in this regard (64.9 %, no significant difference, p-value: > 0.05). The individual performance of the three toolkits are discussed in the following subsections.

5.2.1 Translation of Dislocations by Google

Overall, Google outputs tend to follow the English canonical word order, where the (initial) dislocated item in Persian tends to be translated in its expected canonical position in English. Nevertheless, compared to other toolkits, Google Translate uses more dislocated constituents in its output, especially for reflexive dislocated constituents. Out of the 31 cases of reflexive pronouns, 17 were translated following the Persian word order. For example, من خودم در اصفهان هستم 'I-1st-sg self-1st-sg in Esfahân be-v-pre-1st-sg' has the personal pronouns translated as 'I myself [am in Isfahan]' . We do not have access to Google's training data, but checking the COCA (Corpus of Contemporary American English) and the BNC (British National Corpus), we suggest that the toolkit has a translation which is consistent with observed frequencies, at least in the American English reference corpus: *I myself am* occurs 375 and 15 times, and *I am myself* occurs 125 and 18 times in COCA and BNC, respectively. This may hint that American English might be more present than British English in the training data.

5.2.2 Translation of Dislocations by MBart-50

What is observed in the outputs of MBart-50 is similar to what we have seen in Google Translate. Being closer to the English word order than to the Persian word order may lead to over-translation and sometimes to an incorrect rendering of the source sentence. Some of the examples of dislocations in our data exhibit re-arranging to the English canonical order constituents that are "scrambled" in Persian. Analysing the outputs of MBart-50, we might say that the translation engine does not take into consideration this property of Persian (scrambling), tending to translate sentences strictly following the English word order. Like in this example, گرما رو ازش متنفرم 'heat-râ from-

3sg hate-1sg', the MBart-50 translation *I hate the heat* has 'heat' positioned as object, in its standard SVO position, whereas we may expect 'As for the heat, I hate it' (Azizian et al., 2015) . Topicalization of the object intends to focus addressees' attention on this constituent in the Persian sentence, and the translation by MBart-50 disregards this phenomenon, sticking to the standard word ordering. We could say that the NMT outputs meet syntactic adequacy but not exactly pragmatic adequacy.

5.2.3 Translation of Dislocations by Microsoft Bing

Microsoft Bing records the lowest success rate among our toolkits. This means that it tends to copy the `dislocated` constituents, and it also tries to stick to the English canonical word order. The output for the above-mentioned example م` خودم در اصفهان هستم 'I-1st-sg self-1st-sg in Esfahân be-v-pre-1st-sg' is *I am in Isfahan myself.* Again, the presence of *myself* in final position is frequent in reference corpora (40,265 and 2,141 occurrences in COCA and BNC, respectively, with a high Log likelihood for the American data, 984.96).

Compared to other toolkits, on our (limited) set of examples, Bing produces more nonsense translations for English. In some cases, the very meaning of the source text is ruined. For example, translating the Persian sentence کتابو سامان فرستاد'book-Obj Râ Saman-Sbj send-3sg-pst' (possible translation: *The book, Saman sent.*), Microsoft Bing entirely deteriorates what was said in the source text by the output *Saman's book sent him.* The example clearly indicates that topicalized noun phrase and copy of the same subject in the source sentence can be challenging for the current state of the translation model.

5.2.4 Translation Produced by our Prototype Model

Our translations were far from satisfactory, probably due to data scarcity of training data, though MBART-50 uses only a selection (and a filtered selection) of the TED talk data we used[4]. For MBART-50, they used (after filtering) 14,4895 sentences from TED58 for train, 3,930 for validation and 4,490 sentences for test according to the Appendix of (Tang et al., 2020). Additional data building on Perlex (Asgari-Bidhendi et al., 2021) or exploiting the monolingual BERT for the Persian language (ParsBERT) (Farahani et al., 2021) might be a way to improve the performance of our system.

6 Discussion

6.1 Scrambling and Translations in Fixed Order Languages

Analysing dislocations offers a bird's eye view on a crucial typological distinction between Persian and English. If English has a fixed word order, Persian like some other languages, allows "scrambling", i.e. it has the ability to change word order without changing the meaning (Ross, 1967). The research question can be reformulated, from the point of view of Persian, as "should we pragmatically expect a non-canonical order in the translation?" More generally, does the translation of languages that allow scrambling require a specific word order, for example exploiting Left Periphery? For argument's sake, we investigated the translation of dislocations by MBart-50 into French, which potentially has dislocations, especially in its left periphery. Since French was also included in the 50 languages and is famous for its dislocations, we analysed the outputs in French to see if dislocations were used in the French translations. The copied structures from Persian are not transferred into French in most of the cases. The Persian possessive pronouns are not conveyed in French, and in some other cases, the French output does not make sense, indicating a deficiency in the training process. Hallucinations (Raunak et al., 2021) where outputs are barely related to their source texts can be observed as well as English words in the French translations.

6.2 Pragmatic Adequacy or just Syntactic Adequacy?

Investigating word order in the translation leads us to a more surface analysis of constituents (syntactic adequacy, meeting the requirements of the canonical word order) but paying attention to the possible modifications

[4]To verify our hypothesis, we have trained a second OpenNMT `transformer` model following the same process, by using CCAligned fa↔en parallel corpus as training data, which are 10 times larger than TedTalk corpus. The translations produced by the model are much more relevant.

of the word order leads to a more semantic/pragmatic perspective. Linear arrangement of linguistic elements in a sentence has a role in "processing information and organizing messages at text level" (Baker, 2011). Especially when it comes to spoken data, information structure can be even more complex to capture and interpret. Thus, taking into consideration the *information packaging* of the sentence, including "syntactic, prosodic, and morphological means" plays a crucial role (Vallduví and Engdahl, 1996). Within a text linguistic approach, the clause position is posited as containing a discourse-pragmatic function cross-linguistically. To give an example, the peripheral modifiers in the clause in Persian are placed relatively freely and indicate different discourse functions. In other words, the placement of main and peripheral constituents within a sentence is more determined by semantic and pragmatic factors than by solid rules. In contrast, English syntactic structures are controlled by the grammatical rules. For instance, the constituent that precedes the verb must be subject and the verb must be immediately followed by a direct object (Roberts et al., 2009).

Depending on the position of dislocated constituents within a sentence, we may understand that the speaker tries to introduce a new topic or uses this linguistic device to indicate a contrastive focus. The dislocated constituent might also be used to re-state a given topic for discourse cohesion (Karimi, 2005). We might discuss whether dislocated constructions in the source text should remain a scrambled segment in the target text.

7 Conclusion

In this paper, we have described some existing NLP resources for Persian in relation to Neural Machine Translation. We described how we built our test set extracting examples with the `dislocated` dependency relation from Persian universal dependency treebanks on `GREW`.[5] Though limited in size, it showed issues in more than a third of the translations produced by Google Translate, MBart-50 and Microsoft Bing. The answer to our first research question (do we observe an agrammatical copy of the dislocated item in the translation?) is negative. Our conclusion is that toolkits tend to preserve the canonical structure of an English sentence when it comes to translating Persian dislocated items and topicalized constituents. This partially answers our second research question : the information packaging effect of the dislocation is only partially rendered in the translations.

What is crucial in this challenge set based study is to come up with a challenging structure that is used to probe the NMT toolkits. Dislocation seems a challenging one, since this is not a frequent structure in English. The very question we might ask ourselves is to what extent we expect the system to preserve a dislocated segment in its output. Based on what we have seen in the translations from Persian into English, when the doubled structure does not capture in the translation, the core meaning of the sentence changes. Using a "scrambled" sentence with non-canonical word order, the speaker has a certain purpose. Translating it into the canonical order might ruin the very purpose of the speaker and might not convey the exact state-of-affairs in discourse. Thus, to reach pragmatic adequacy, it might be suggested that the dislocated item in Persian be given a specific status in information structure in the target sentence. It might be excessive to suggest that we should expect the systems to produce a sentence preserving the non-canonical structure of the source text. Since dislocations are mostly used in spoken data, we can suggest that systems are probably not sufficiently trained with this type of data. In this sense, to align with frequent structures in spoken data, our challenge set could be expanded using other grammatical phenomena such as *it*-clefts and pseudo-clefts or to include cases of local scrambling and long distance scrambling (Rezaei, 2000).

Acknowledgments

This publication has emanated from research supported in part by the 2020 "émergence" research project SPECTRANS, under the ANR grant (ANR-18-IDEX-0001, Financement IdEx Université Paris Cité).

[5] We completed our test set of 57 examples, to be found on `https://github.com/nballier/SPECTRANS/tree/main/NSUR` with examples from (Yousef and Torabi, 2021) and (Azizian et al., 2015).

References

Jan W Amtrup, Hamid Mansouri Rad, Karine Megerdoomian, and Rémi Zajac. 2000. Persian-English machine translation: An overview of the shiraz project. *Memoranda in Computer and Cognitive Science MCCS-00-319, NMSU, CRL.*

Majid Asgari-Bidhendi, Mehrdad Nasser, Behrooz Janfada, and Behrouz Minaei-Bidgoli. 2021. Perlex: A bilingual Persian-English gold dataset for relation extraction. *Scientific Programming*, 2021.

Yunes Azizian, Arsalan Golfam, and Aliye Kord-e Zafaranlu Kambuziya. 2015. A construction grammar account of left dislocation in persian. *Mediterranean Journal of Social Sciences*, 6(6 S2):98.

Mona Baker. 2011. *In Other Words: A Coursebook on Translation.* Taylor & Francis.

Ondřej Bojar, Rajen Chatterjee, Christian Federmann, Barry Haddow, Matthias Huck, Chris Hokamp, Philipp Koehn, Varvara Logacheva, Christof Monz, Matteo Negri, Matt Post, Carolina Scarton, Lucia Specia, and Marco Turchi. 2015. Findings of the 2015 workshop on statistical machine translation. In *Proceedings of the Tenth Workshop on Statistical Machine Translation*, pages 1–46, Lisbon, Portugal. Association for Computational Linguistics.

Guillaume Bonfante, Bruno Guillaume, and Guy Perrier. 2018. *Application of Graph Rewriting to Natural Language Processing.* John Wiley & Sons.

Marie-Catherine De Marneffe, Bill MacCartney, Christopher D Manning, et al. 2006. Generating typed dependency parses from phrase structure parses. In *LREC*, volume 6, pages 449–454.

Marie-Catherine De Marneffe and Christopher D Manning. 2008. The Stanford typed dependencies representation. In *Coling 2008: proceedings of the workshop on cross-framework and cross-domain parser evaluation*, pages 1–8.

Ahmed El-Kishky, Vishrav Chaudhary, Francisco Guzmán, and Philipp Koehn. 2020. CCAligned: A massive collection of cross-lingual web-document pairs. In *Proceedings of the 2020 Conference on Empirical Methods in Natural Language Processing (EMNLP 2020).*

Pegah Faghiri and Pollet Samvelian. 2021. A corpus-based description of cleft constructions in Persian. *Faits de langues*, pages 183—206. Palancar, Enrique & Martine Vanhove (eds.).

Mehrdad Farahani, Mohammad Gharachorloo, Marzieh Farahani, and Mohammad Manthouri. 2021. ParsBERT: Transformer-based model for Persian language understanding. *Neural Processing Letters*, 53(6):3831–3847.

Abed Alhakim Freihat and Mourad Abbas. 2021. Proceedings of the second international workshop on nlp solutions for under resourced languages (nsurl 2021) co-located with icnlsp 2021. In *Proceedings of The Second International Workshop on NLP Solutions for Under Resourced Languages (NSURL 2021) co-located with ICNLSP 2021.*

Gaël Guibon, Marine Courtin, Kim Gerdes, and Bruno Guillaume. 2020. When collaborative treebank curation meets graph grammars. In *Proceedings of The 12th Language Resources and Evaluation Conference*, pages 5293–5302, Marseille, France. European Language Resources Association.

Lifeng Han, Alan Smeaton, and Gareth Jones. 2021. Translation quality assessment: A brief survey on manual and automatic methods. In *Proceedings for the First Workshop on Modelling Translation: Translatology in the Digital Age*, pages 15–33, online. Association for Computational Linguistics.

Matthew Honnibal and Mark Johnson. 2015. An improved non-monotonic transition system for dependency parsing. In *Proceedings of the 2015 Conference on Empirical Methods in Natural Language Processing*, pages 1373–1378, Lisbon, Portugal. Association for Computational Linguistics.

Pierre Isabelle, Colin Cherry, and George Foster. 2017. A challenge set approach to evaluating machine translation. *Proceedings of the 2017 Conference on Empirical Methods in Natural Language Processing*, pages 2486—2496.

S. Karimi. 2005. *A Minimalist Approach to Scrambling: Evidence from Persian.* Studies in generative grammar. Mouton de Gruyter.

Omid Kashefi. 2018. Mizan: A large Persian-English parallel corpus.

Guillaume Klein, Yoon Kim, Yuntian Deng, Jean Senellart, and Alexander Rush. 2017. OpenNMT: Open-source toolkit for neural machine translation. In *Proceedings of ACL 2017, System Demonstrations*, pages 67–72, Vancouver, Canada. Association for Computational Linguistics.

Taku Kudo. 2018. Subword regularization: Improving neural network translation models with multiple subword candidates. In *Proceedings of the 56th Annual Meeting of the Association for Computational Linguistics (Volume 1: Long Papers)*, pages 66–75, Melbourne, Australia. Association for Computational Linguistics.

Mahsa Mohaghegh. 2012. *English-Persian phrase-based statistical machine translation: enhanced models, search and training: a thesis presented in fulfilment of the requirements for the degree of Doctor of Philosophy in Computer Engineering at Massey University, Albany (Auckland), New Zealand.* Ph.D. thesis, Massey University.

Behnoosh Namdarzadeh and Nicolas Ballier. 2022. The neural machine translation of dislocations. *ExLing 2022*, 28:127–131.

Peng Qi, Timothy Dozat, Yuhao Zhang, and Christopher D. Manning. 2018. Universal dependency parsing from scratch. In *Proceedings of the CoNLL 2018 Shared Task: Multilingual Parsing from Raw Text to Universal Dependencies*, pages 160–170, Brussels, Belgium. Association for Computational Linguistics.

Peng Qi, Yuhao Zhang, Yuhui Zhang, Jason Bolton, and Christopher D Manning. 2020. Stanza: A python natural language processing toolkit for many human languages. *arXiv preprint arXiv:2003.07082*.

R Core Team. 2022. *R: A Language and Environment for Statistical Computing*. R Foundation for Statistical Computing, Vienna, Austria.

Mohammad Sadegh Rasooli, Manouchehr Kouhestani, and Amirsaeid Moloodi. 2013. Development of a Persian syntactic dependency treebank. In *Proceedings of the 2013 Conference of the North American Chapter of the Association for Computational Linguistics: Human Language Technologies*, pages 306–314, Atlanta, Georgia. Association for Computational Linguistics.

Mohammad Sadegh Rasooli, Pegah Safari, Amirsaeid Moloodi, and Alireza Nourian. 2020. The Persian dependency treebank made universal. *arXiv preprint arXiv:2009.10205*.

Vikas Raunak, Arul Menezes, and Marcin Junczys-Dowmunt. 2021. The curious case of hallucinations in neural machine translation. In *Proceedings of the 2021 Conference of the North American Chapter of the Association for Computational Linguistics: Human Language Technologies*, pages 1172–1183, Online. Association for Computational Linguistics.

Nils Reimers and Iryna Gurevych. 2020. Making monolingual sentence embeddings multilingual using knowledge distillation. In *Proceedings of the 2020 Conference on Empirical Methods in Natural Language Processing (EMNLP)*, pages 4512–4525, Online. Association for Computational Linguistics.

Siamak Rezaei. 2000. *Linguistic and computational analysis of word order and scrambling in Persian.* Ph.D. thesis, University of Edinburgh. College of Science and Engineering.

John Richard Roberts, Behrooz Barjasteh Delforooz, and Carina Jahani. 2009. A Study of Persian Discourse Structure. Uppsala University Library.

John Robert Ross. 1967. *Constraints on Variables in Syntax.* Ph.D. thesis, MIT.

Mojgan Seraji. 2015. *Morphosyntactic corpora and tools for Persian.* Ph.D. thesis, Acta Universitatis Upsaliensis.

Mojgan Seraji, Filip Ginter, and Joakim Nivre. 2016. Universal dependencies for persian. In *Proceedings of the Tenth International Conference on Language Resources and Evaluation (LREC'16)*, pages 2361–2365.

Yuqing Tang, Chau Tran, Xian Li, Peng-Jen Chen, Naman Goyal, Vishrav Chaudhary, Jiatao Gu, and Angela Fan. 2020. Multilingual translation with extensible multilingual pretraining and finetuning.

Jörg Tiedemann. 2016. OPUS – Parallel corpora for everyone. In *Proceedings of the 19th Annual Conference of the European Association for Machine Translation: Projects/Products*, Riga, Latvia. Baltic Journal of Modern Computing.

Enric Vallduví and Elisabet Engdahl. 1996. The Linguistic realization of information packaging. *Linguistics*, 34(3):459–520.

Jan Wijffels. 2022. *udpipe: Tokenization, Parts of Speech Tagging, Lemmatization and Dependency Parsing with the 'UDPipe' 'NLP' Toolkit.* R package version 0.8.9.

S. Yousef and H. Torabi. 2021. *Intermediate Persian: A Grammar and Workbook.* Routledge Grammar Workbooks. Taylor & Francis.

Mina Zand Rahimi, Moein Madayenzadeh, and Mahdi Alizadeh. 2017. A comparative study of english-persian translation of neural google translation. *Iranian Journal of Applied Language Studies*, 9(Proceedings of the First International Conference on Language Focus):279–286.

Love Me, Love Me Not:
Human-Directed Sentiment Analysis in Arabic

Abraham Israeli,[1,2] Aviv Naaman,[1] Yotam Nahum,[1] Razan Assi,[3] Shai Fine,[1] Kfir Bar[1]
[1]The Data Science Institute, Arabic NLP Lab, Reichman University, Israel
[2]Ben-Gurion University of the Negev, Israel
[3]Hebrew University of Jerusalem, Israel
{abraham.israeli,aviv.naaman,yotam.nahum,kfir.bar}@post.idc.ac.il,
razan.assi@mail.huji.ac.il
shai.fine@idc.ac.il

Abstract

Gauging the emotions people have toward a specific topic is a major natural language processing task, supporting various applications. The topic can be either an abstract idea (e.g., religion) or a service/product that someone writes a review about. In this work, we define the topic to be a person who writes a post on a social media platform. More precisely, we introduce a new sentiment analysis task for detecting the sentiment that is expressed by a user toward another user in a discussion thread. Modeling this new task may be beneficial for various applications, including hate-speech detection, and cyber-bullying mitigation. We focus on Arabic, which is one of the most popular spoken languages worldwide, divided into various dialects that are used on social media platforms. We compose a corpus of 3,500 pairs of tweets, with the second tweet being a response to the first one, and manually annotate them for the sentiment that is expressed in the response toward the author of the main tweet. We train several baseline models and discuss their results and limitations. The best classification result that we recorded is 82% F1 score. We release the corpus alongside the best-performing model.

1 Introduction

Sentiment analysis (SA) is one of the most popular tasks in natural language processing (NLP). It is the task of classifying a given piece of text according to the emotions expressed by its author. In its simplest form, the sentiment is classified as positive, negative, or neutral. Aspect-based sentiment analysis (ABSA), a variant of sentiment analysis, is the task of mining opinions from texts, expressed toward specific entities and their aspects (Cambria et al., 2013). For example, in the following review: "`Nice restaurant, a bit expensive but the food is great`", the entity is the restaurant and the aspects are the price and quality of food. While the author writes positively about the quality of food, he/she has some reservations about the price. ABSA is considered an active research area (Pontiki et al., 2016; Ma et al., 2019; Zhang and Qian, 2020; Zhang et al., 2021; Li et al., 2021). However, most of the studies are done with texts written in English.

In the last two decades, social networks have become the dominant written-communication platforms.[1] In most platforms, the users may engage with other posts by up-voting, also known as "like", and by replying with a nested post, thereby generating a discussion thread, open for all users. Most of the existing computational methods for SA do not encode this conversational structure into their prediction models.

With the recent growing interest in training NLP models for languages other than English, the Arabic language has become one of the most prominent among research groups. (Bouamor et al., 2018; Obeid et al., 2020). Nonetheless, the amount of effort invested in advancing sentiment-related technologies in Arabic, is still considered limited comparing to English (Farha and Magdy, 2019; Guellil et al., 2019; Abu Farha et al., 2021; Alhumoud and Al Wazrah, 2021). Therefore, in this work we have opted to work on Arabic, a Semitic language, highly inflected for different lingustic categories. Arabic has what is usually referred to as diglossia, which is a separation between the written and the spoken language. Modern Standard Arabic (MSA) is the language that people use in official settings, while spoken Arabic is considered to be a collection of regional dialects that may significantly differ from each other. In informal writing people often mix MSA with the relevant dialect, forming what is called Middle Arabic. Arabic tweets are typically written in that Middle Arabic, which is in fact described on a spectrum ranging from MSA to the relevant regional dialect. In this work, we

[1]Facebook reported on 2.9 Billion monthly active users (retrieved 09/12/2022), see: https://tinyurl.com/52h8b4mb

put a special focus on tweets written in a mixture of MSA and the Levantine dialects,[2] which are mostly spoken in Lebanon, Syria, Israel, Palestine, and Jordan.

In Section 6, we further elaborate on our future plans to expand this work to other dialects and potentially to other languages.

In this paper, we present a new sentiment analysis task, somewhat related to ABSA, which is about detecting the sentiment expressed by a user toward another user in a discussion thread. We call this task "human-directed sentiment analysis" (`HD-Sentiment`). The emotions that users express toward other users, may play an important role for many NLP applications, such as hate-speech detection (Waseem and Hovy, 2016; Mondal et al., 2017; Ziems et al., 2020), cyber-bullying (Whittaker and Kowalski, 2015; Rosa et al., 2019), and user-based recommendation systems (Han and Karypis, 2005; Da'u and Salim, 2020). To the best of our knowledge, this is the first study to define the `HD-Sentiment` task and to provide a manually annotated corpus that can be used computationally. Similar to other sentiment analysis tasks, we work with three labels: positive, negative, and neutral. To simplify the task, we define it to have an input composed of a pair of posts, the *main post* and the *response*, rather than the entire discussion thread. The goal of the task is to detect the sentiment expressed by the responder in the response post, toward the author of the main post. The model can only use the texts of both posts as input. Adding information to the input will be considered in future works. Figure 1 shows an example of such a pair of posts, written by two different users. In this example, it is clear that the sentiment expressed by the responder toward the author of the main post is positive.

In accordance with other ABSA-related corpora, while the overall sentiment expressed by the responder can be positive, the sentiment toward the main author can be expressed as negative.

`HD-Sentiment` is related to dialogue-level sentiment analysis (Li et al., 2017; Chen et al., 2018; Zhang et al., 2020) since the sentiment is expressed toward participants in a multi-user conversation. `HD-Sentiment` can be of special interest to dialogue-level sentiment researchers as this aspect of the conversation sheds light on the relations between users, which are yet to be addressed. Due to

[2] Both Northern and Southern Levantine dialects.

Figure 1: Example of a tweet and a response. We conceal all identities to preserve users' right to remain anonymous. The example was captured along with an English translation, suggested originally by Google Translate. In this example, we label the human-directed sentiment (`HD-Sentiment`) as positive.

the way the data were collected and annotated (see Section 3), we prefer to define `HD-Sentiment` as a special case of ABSA rather than a sub-topic within dialogue-level sentiment analysis.

At a first glance, the `HD-Sentiment` task seems fairly easy, especially for a response that looks like this: "`@[USER] I admire you`". However, many times responders tend to express their feelings implicitly, using humor, sarcasm, and other figures of speech. The nature of the platform may also affect the way people express themselves in posts (Fiesler et al., 2018). For example, Twitter is a platform for short messages, which forces people to depend on the broader context and compress their messages accordingly.

Table 1 provides some examples of pairs of posts and responses, taken from the corpus we are releasing with this work. The tweets were originally written in Arabic; we added English translations for convenience. For each pair, we provide the label that was assigned by a human annotator, reflecting the sentiment expressed by the responder toward the author of the main post. More details about the corpus are discussed in Section 3.1. Notably, some examples are more explicit than others. They use words that explicitly express emotions, as well as direct references to the author of the main post (e.g., first row). However, in other tweets it is harder to interpret the underlying sentiment. In the third row, it is due to the sarcastic style that is used by the responders. Additionally, like with other ABSA tasks, there are cases where the author does not refer to the aspect at all. The example in the second row is labeled as neutral since there is no evidence for addressing the main author (equivalent to the aspect in ABSA). However, even when explicitly referring to the main authors, responses do not necessarily convey emotions toward them.

Our contribution is threefold: (i) We define a new NLP sentiment analysis task, `HD-Sentiment`; (ii) We release the first annotated corpus designed for the `HD-Sentiment` task, consisting of 3.5K Arabic-written tweets. The dataset is available for download.[3]; and (iii) We report on some baseline results of models that we train for the task. We make the best model available for public use in the HuggingFace public repository.[4]

2 Related Work

Sentiment analysis has been an active research area in the past few decades (Agarwal et al., 2011; Rosenthal et al., 2017a; Sandoval-Almazan and Valle-Cruz, 2018; Lindskog and Serur, 2020). Commonly, an SA task is designed as a binary classification for positive/negative labels. There are a number of popular data sets for the binary classification version, such as IMDb (Maas et al., 2011), consisting of 50K reviews from the Internet Movie Database (IMDb), as well as the Stanford Sentiment Treebank 2 (SST-2) (Socher et al., 2013), which contains about 200K movie reviews. Another known data set is the Yelp Reviews (Asghar, 2016), consisting of more than 500K reviews.

Twitter has always been one of the main sources for acquiring data for SA, exposing some additional information about every tweet and the users beyond the plain text. The SemEval Workshop has a special track for sentiment analysis. Specifically, SemEval-2017 Task 4 (Rosenthal et al., 2017b) consists of five subtasks representing different variants of SA for tweets, written in English and Arabic. Subtask B is about classifying the sentiment expressed in the tweet toward a given topic.

There are a few data sets for the aspect-based SA (ABSA) task. The SemEval-2016 task is the most dominant one (Pontiki et al., 2016). It consists of four subtasks, which vary from the detection of the relevant aspects in the text to the detection of the polarity of a given aspect. The data set contains about 6K reviews.

Considering the information about the author of the input text has been a point of interest, as described several times. Tang et al. (2015) defined a task of SA on reviews in which the user who wrote the text, as well as the product for which the text is written for, are given as input. In another work (Welch and Mihalcea, 2016), a new task has been defined for understanding the sentiment that students hold toward courses and instructors, as expressed by students in their comments. Equivalently, in our work, we are interested in the sentiment that is expressed in a reply tweet, toward the author of the original tweet.

In this work, we focus on Arabic-written tweets. There is a surging amount of computational works on Arabic, especially works related to SA on tweets (Nabil et al., 2015; Abdellaoui and Zrigui, 2018) as well as on other genres (Al-Obaidi and Samawi, 2016). In a recent work (Al-Laith et al., 2021), there has been an attempt to automatically build a large corpus of Arabic texts, annotated for SA. None of these corpora address the task that we define in this work.

3 Data Collection

In this work, we collect data from Twitter. Twitter allows users to reply to posts written by other users. We use the official Twitter API to collect conversation threads of tweets and replies. We define a set of 61 Arabic expressions to limit our collection for tweets that are relevant to the area and dialect of interest. The expressions were carefully composed to cover a variety of topics, such as sports, politics, and economics. Table 2 lists some of them. Additionally, we compile a list of relevant Twitter accounts, known for writing posts with high engagement rates. Most of them are key opinion leaders (e.g., Saad Hariri who was the prime minister of Lebanon). The full list of expressions, as well as the Twitter accounts that we used, is released with the corpus.[5]

The collection was done in June 2021 and applied a full-archive crawling procedure, so the crawling procedure is essentially unlimited by time.

We filtered out conversation threads that *do not* meet at least one of the following three criteria: (i) The tweet language is predominantly Arabic. (ii) The main post contains more than ten characters. (iii) There are at least ten responses to the main post.

[3]https://github.com/idc-dsi/Human-Directed-Sentiment

[4]https://huggingface.co/DSI/human-directed-sentiment

[5]https://github.com/idc-dsi/Human-Directed-Sentiment

	Main Post	Response Post	L
1	اذا وصلت لمرحلة إنك ترى وتعرف كل شيء ولكنك تظهر لهم إنك غبي ولم تفهم شيء فأنت قد فهمت الحياة تماماً.. 😉 #صباحو_للعالم_بتدّعي_الذكا 😪 If you reach the stage in which you see and know everything but act as if you are ignorant and don't understand anything then you have fully understood life..😉 #Good Morning to the people who pretend to be smart 😪	دخل ذكاكي انت 😍😍 How clever you are 😍😍	POS
2	هذه الليلة توفي دونالد رامسفيلد، أحد معدي ومخططي اجتياح افغانستان والعراق .هو أحد أهم الرجال الدمويين في إدارة جورج بوش الإبن. Tonight, Donald Rumsfeld, one of the organizers and planners of the invasions of Afghanistan and Iraq, died. He is one of the most important and bloody men in the administration of George Bush Jr.	اليوم يسلم كتابه بشماله.. عند رب يقول انا منا نستنسخ ما كنتم تعملون ..ويقول في كتاب لا يغادر صغيرة ولا كبيرة إلا احصاها ...اليوم يرى عين الحقيقة المطلقة للآخرة Today he returns his soul... Facing the Lord he says, "I will not reproduce what you did." He will tell it all, big and small. Today he faces the eternal truth	NEU
3	الرئيس عون: ما حصل في الأيام الماضية أمام محطات المحروقات غير مقبول، وإذلال المواطنين مرفوض تحت أي اعتبار، وعلى جميع المعنيين العمل على منع تكرار هذه الممارسات سيّما وانّ جدولاً جديداً لأسعار المحروقات صدر، ومن شأنه أن يخفّف الأزمة President Aoun: What happened in the past few days in front of the gas stations is unacceptable, and the humiliation of citizens is rejected under any consideration, and all concerned should work to prevent the recurrence of these practices, especially since a new tariff of fuel prices has been issued, which would alleviate the crisis.	صرلو فترة هيك لازم تضرب ايدك عالطاولة وتقله لرئيس الجمهورية يحسن الوضع شوي It's been like that for some time, you ought to hit your fist on the table and tell the President of the Republic to make things a little better.	NEG

Table 1: Examples of pairs of a post and response. The examples are taken from our annotated corpus. POS, NEU, and NEG are the positive, neutral, and negative labels respectively. We added English translations, which were manually prepared by a native speaker.

Overall, we collected 20.1K threads, corresponding to a total number of 346.3K tweets.

As mentioned above, instead of working with full conversation threads, we define our task to focus only on pairs of tweets, the main post, and one of its responses. Therefore, we compile our corpus accordingly.

Expression	Translation	Domain
الامير حمزة	Prince Hamzah	Politics
فلسطين	Palestine	Politics
ارتفاع الاسعار	High Prices	Economics
اصوات من السماء	Voices from Heaven	Religious
بشار مراد	Bashar Murad[6]	Culture
جميلة عوض	Jamila Awad[7]	Culture

[6] A Palestinian singer, songwriter, and social activist.
[7] An Egyptian actress.

Table 2: Crawling expressions. A *sample* of the Arabic terms we use for crawling, provided with their English translation, and the domain they are most relevant to.

	Main Posts			Response Posts		
	Avg.	Med.	Std.	Avg.	Med.	Std.
Chars	175.12	179	83.41	109.16	85	73.11
Tokens	64.85	65	30.34	43.25	35	27.09
Hashtags	0.53	0	1.09	0.11	0	0.56
Emojis	0.01	0	0.12	0.45	0	0.68

Table 3: Corpus statistics. The numbers are calculated over the entire collection of 3,500 tweets. Avg., Med., and Std. are the average, median, and standard deviation respectively.

3.1 Human Annotation

We sampled 3,500 pairs uniformly from the main collection of conversational threads, and assigned them for human annotation. Specifically, we pair every main post with up to five responses, chosen randomly. We provide some additional information about the chosen tweets in Table 3. We learn from the table that main posts are significantly longer than responses. Additionally, the authors of the main posts tend to use hashtags more frequently than responders, while the latter use emojis in their tweets more than main authors do.

We hired three human annotators to label the 3,500 tweet pairs. All annotators are highly educated Arabic speakers, fluent in MSA and the relevant regional dialects. They were introduced to the definition of the task, and were given careful annotation guidelines alongside specific annotation examples. As a first phase, we started annotating a small set of 100 pairs for training the annotators and calibrating the guidelines. The guidelines were adjusted to handle cases of annotator disagreements. In the second phase, we asked two annotators to label the entire set of 3,500 pairs. The agreement of the two annotators was measured to be 74%, corresponding to a kappa (Cohen, 1960) value of 0.59. The third annotator was assigned with the adjudication task, where he was asked to label only pairs on which the two annotators disagreed (26% of the pairs), to have a final decision for each pair.

In 95.3% of the cases, the third annotator agreed with one of the annotators. For our final corpus we removed the pairs that had complete disagreement among all three annotators (43 cases). The distribution of the [positive, neutral, negative] labels in the corpus are [9.59%, 44.45%, 45.95%]. We believe that the relatively small number of positive pairs stems from the nature of the platform as well as the topics and geography that we decided to focus on.

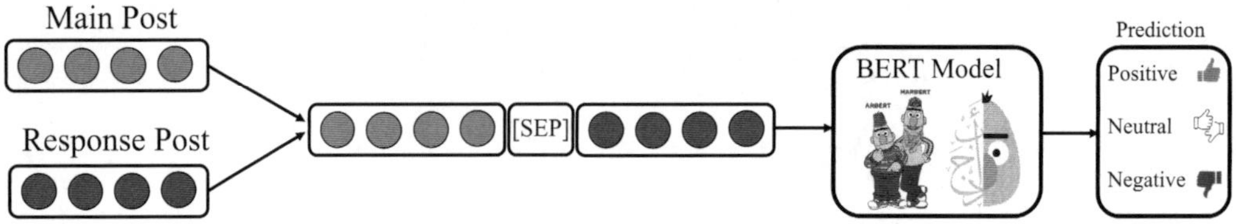

Figure 2: Our architecture for the fine-tuned BERT-based models. We concatenate the main post and the response and add the special token [SEP] in between.

4 Computational Approach

To validate the new annotated dataset and its usability, we trained three classifiers and compared their performance with two baseline approaches.

4.1 Experimental Setting

We preprocessed every tweet by replacing user mentions (formatted in Twitter as @<user>) with a placeholder word `[USER]`, and urls with `[URL]`. Hashtags remain untouched, as they may carry important information for SA. For evaluation, we used a 5-fold cross-validation approach. To get the most out of the new annotated resource, and due to the low support for the positive label, we do not split the corpus for train and test sets. We use the standard classification evaluation metrics. For each label, we calculate the precision, recall, and F1-score, as well as the macro and weighted-average scores over the three labels.

We fine-tuned different Arabic BERT (Devlin et al., 2019) models on the new `HD-Sentiment` corpus, during 5 epochs. To handle the skewed distribution of the labels, we used a weighted cross-entropy loss, with weights assigned according to the inverse proportion of their distribution.

4.2 BERT Based Classifiers

We preprocessed every input pair of tweets by concatenating the main post and the response with a special [SEP] token placed in between. The full architecture of our model is depicted in Figure 2. We used three different pre-trained Arabic language models,[8] using the transformers (Wolf et al., 2020) library by Hugging Face[9]: `AraBERT` (Antoun et al., 2020), `GigaBERT` (Lan et al., 2020), and `MARBERT` (Abdul-Mageed et al., 2020) that relies solely on Twitter data, which makes it a better fit for NLP tasks involving dialectical Arabic texts from social media, such as ours.

[8]Using the `BertForSequenceClassification` class.

[9]https://huggingface.co

4.3 Baseline models

We compared our classifiers with two baselines:

CAMeLBERT Sentiment Analysis. CAMeLBERT (Inoue et al., 2021) is a pre-trained language model, which has already been fine-tuned for several downstream Arabic NLP tasks, including sentiment analysis.[10] By the time of writing this paper, it is considered to deliver state-of-art results for SA in Arabic. The model was trained to classify texts with three labels: positive, negative, and neutral. We run the model on the response tweet to gauge its overall sentiment, which we return as a final predicted label.

Lexicon-Based Model. First, we look for mentions of the main author in the response, including references through 2nd-person pronouns. If none are found, the model returns "neutral". However, if found, we use existing lexicons (Saif M. Mohammad and Kiritchenko, 2016) for detecting all instances of emotional words and related hashtags. Every word is assigned with a sentiment score,[11] which we average into an overall sentiment score assigned for the response. We predict "positive" (or "negative") based on the sign of the overall score.

5 Results and Analysis

The results obtained by each model averaged over the five cross-validation folds, are summarized in Table 4. The best results in each column are in boldface. We add $*$ next to a number to indicate statistically significant results (p-value $< 10^{-4}$), using the Mann Whitney U-test (Mann and Whitney, 1947). The first two rows are the results of the baseline models (see Section 4.3). While the baseline models show competitive results in some of the individual labels, their overall results (measured as macro-F1 (M-F1) and weighted-F1 (W-F1)) are much worse than the results obtained by the fine-tuned models.

[10]CAMeL-Lab/bert-base-arabic-camelbert-da-sentiment

[11]The score is not limited to a specific value range, which can also be negative

	Positive			Neutral			Negative			All	
	P	R	F1	P	R	F1	P	R	F1	M-F1	W-F1
Lexicon	0.11	0.52	0.19	0.74	0.67	0.7	0.6	0.21	0.31	0.4±0.01	0.48±0.01
CAMeLB	0.39	**0.68**	0.49	0.77	0.11	0.19	0.55	**0.91***	0.69	0.46±0.02	0.45±0.01
AraBERT	0.62	0.14	0.22	0.75	0.71	0.72	0.69	0.83	0.75	0.57±0.05	0.69±0.02
GigaBERT	**0.8**	0.3	0.43	0.78	0.77	0.78	0.74	0.84	0.78	0.66±0.04	0.75±0.02
MARBERT	0.79	0.67	**0.72***	**0.84***	**0.81***	**0.82***	**0.82***	0.87	**0.84***	**0.79 ± 0.02***	**0.82 ± 0.02***

Table 4: Results. P and R are precision and recall. M-F1 and W-F1 are the macro-F1 and weighted-F1 over the three labels. Lexicon and CAMelB are the lexicon-based and CAMeLBERT Sentiment Analysis models, respectively. Results are averaged over the five cross-validation folds. The standard deviation of the overall results is provided in the last two columns. The best results are in boldface while the second-best results are underlined. Statistically significant best results are marked with a *.

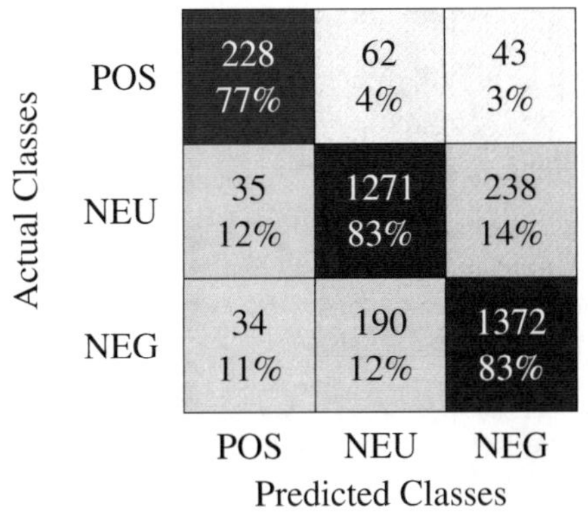

Figure 3: Confusion matrix for the best performing model (MARBERT). POS, NEU, and NEG are the positive, neutral, and negative labels, respectively. The percentage number in each cell is calculated columnwise.

Among the fine-tuned models, both AraBERT and GigaBERT perform well on the neutral and negative labels. However, their performance on the positive label, the one with the low support, is not as good. On the other hand, MARBERT outperforms all other models, on all labels' F1 scores as well as on the aggregated overall scores. This is unsurprising, considering that MARBERT was trained solely on Twitter data, and its size is larger than the other models' datasets.

We now take a closer look into the performance of the MARBERT model. Figure 3 is the confusion matrix we got by running MARBERT on the five cross-validation folds. It looks like the model has hard time distinguishing between the neutral and negative labels. On the other hand, the negative and positive labels are rarely "mixed up" by the model. As observed in both Table 4 and Figure 3, positive is the most difficult label to predict.

Quantitative analysis. Overall there are 602 misclassified pairs, out of which 317 (52.7%) were assigned with two different labels by the original human annotators. Disagreement at a rate of 52.7% is significantly higher than the disagreement rate of the entire corpus (26%, see Section 3.1), suggesting that the misclassified pairs are likely to be more difficult than the others even for human annotators.

6 Conclusion and Future Work

In this work we defined a new task, called Human-Directed Sentiment Analysis (`HD-Sentiment`). We collected and annotated the first `HD-Sentiment` corpus, and made it publicly available. Additionally, we fine-tuned a number of baseline models, discussed their results, and published the one that performed best.

`HD-Sentiment` may be considered as a special case of ABSA using only one aspect defined as the author of the main post. To some extent, `HD-Sentiment` extends previous works in the field of hate-speech detection and cyber-bullying; however, `HD-Sentiment` is more general as it aims at capturing a full range of emotions expressed in conversations, which are neither considered as bullying nor as expressing hate towards someone.

Part of the challenge in `HD-Sentiment` is the fact that the users who are involved in the conversations are not necessarily known in advance and are not provided as input to the learning model. We do not store historical information about the users nor their previous interactions. In our corpus, we included interactions between users, who may or may not know each other in advance.

Finally, we decided to work with Arabic, one of the most popular spoken languages worldwide.Consequently, there is a growing interest in processing Arabic for various NLP tasks. However, we believe that the `HD-Sentiment` task can be applied in other languages and other social platforms.

Future work takes two trajectories: (i) Extending `HD-Sentiment` to other languages, including the collection and annotation of additional corpora, and (ii) Building an explainability component for `HD-Sentiment` classifiers to better interpret the model's output.

References

Houssem Abdellaoui and Mounir Zrigui. 2018. Using tweets and emojis to build tead: an arabic dataset for sentiment analysis. *Computación y Sistemas*, 22(3):777–786.

Muhammad Abdul-Mageed, AbdelRahim Elmadany, and El Moatez Billah Nagoudi. 2020. Arbert & marbert: Deep bidirectional transformers for arabic. *arXiv preprint arXiv:2101.01785*.

Ibrahim Abu Farha, Wajdi Zaghouani, and Walid Magdy. 2021. Overview of the wanlp 2021 shared task on sarcasm and sentiment detection in arabic. In *Proceedings of the Sixth Arabic Natural Language Processing Workshop*.

Apoorv Agarwal, Boyi Xie, Ilia Vovsha, Owen Rambow, and Rebecca J Passonneau. 2011. Sentiment analysis of twitter data. In *Proceedings of the workshop on language in social media (LSM 2011)*, pages 30–38.

Ali Al-Laith, Muhammad Shahbaz, Hind F Alaskar, and Asim Rehmat. 2021. Arasencorpus: A semi-supervised approach for sentiment annotation of a large arabic text corpus. *Applied Sciences*, 11(5):2434.

Ahmed Y Al-Obaidi and Venus W Samawi. 2016. Opinion mining: analysis of comments written in arabic colloquial. In *Proceedings of the World Congress on Engineering and Computer Science*, volume 1.

Sarah Omar Alhumoud and Asma Ali Al Wazrah. 2021. Arabic sentiment analysis using recurrent neural networks: a review. *Artificial Intelligence Review*, pages 1–42.

Wissam Antoun, Fady Baly, and Hazem Hajj. 2020. Arabert: Transformer-based model for arabic language understanding. *arXiv preprint arXiv:2003.00104*.

Nabiha Asghar. 2016. Yelp dataset challenge: Review rating prediction. *arXiv preprint arXiv:1605.05362*.

Houda Bouamor, Nizar Habash, Mohammad Salameh, Wajdi Zaghouani, Owen Rambow, Dana Abdulrahim, Ossama Obeid, Salam Khalifa, Fadhl Eryani, Alexander Erdmann, et al. 2018. The madar arabic dialect corpus and lexicon. In *Proceedings of the Eleventh International Conference on Language Resources and Evaluation (LREC 2018)*.

Erik Cambria, Björn Schuller, Yunqing Xia, and Catherine Havasi. 2013. New avenues in opinion mining and sentiment analysis. *IEEE Intelligent systems*, 28(2):15–21.

Sheng-Yeh Chen, Chao-Chun Hsu, Chuan-Chun Kuo, Lun-Wei Ku, et al. 2018. Emotionlines: An emotion corpus of multi-party conversations. *arXiv preprint arXiv:1802.08379*.

Jacob Cohen. 1960. A coefficient of agreement for nominal scales. *Educational and psychological measurement*, 20(1):37–46.

Aminu Da'u and Naomie Salim. 2020. Recommendation system based on deep learning methods: a systematic review and new directions. *Artificial Intelligence Review*, 53(4):2709–2748.

Jacob Devlin, Ming-Wei Chang, Kenton Lee, and Kristina Toutanova. 2019. BERT: Pre-training of deep bidirectional transformers for language understanding. In *Proceedings of the 2019 Conference of the North American Chapter of the Association for Computational Linguistics: Human Language Technologies, Volume 1 (Long and Short Papers)*, pages 4171–4186, Minneapolis, Minnesota. Association for Computational Linguistics.

Ibrahim Abu Farha and Walid Magdy. 2019. Mazajak: An online arabic sentiment analyser. In *Proceedings of the Fourth Arabic Natural Language Processing Workshop*, pages 192–198.

Casey Fiesler, Joshua McCann, Kyle Frye, Jed R Brubaker, et al. 2018. Reddit rules! characterizing an ecosystem of governance. In *Twelfth International AAAI Conference on Web and Social Media*.

Imane Guellil, Faical Azouaou, and Marcelo Mendoza. 2019. Arabic sentiment analysis: studies, resources, and tools. *Social Network Analysis and Mining*, 9(1):1–17.

Eui-Hong Han and George Karypis. 2005. Feature-based recommendation system. In *Proceedings of the 14th ACM international conference on Information and knowledge management*, pages 446–452.

Go Inoue, Bashar Alhafni, Nurpeiis Baimukan, Houda Bouamor, and Nizar Habash. 2021. The interplay of variant, size, and task type in arabic pre-trained language models. *arXiv preprint arXiv:2103.06678*.

Wuwei Lan, Yang Chen, Wei Xu, and Alan Ritter. 2020. Gigabert: Zero-shot transfer learning from english to arabic. In *Proceedings of The 2020 Conference on Empirical Methods on Natural Language Processing (EMNLP)*.

Ruifan Li, Hao Chen, Fangxiang Feng, Zhanyu Ma, Xiaojie Wang, and Eduard Hovy. 2021. Dual graph convolutional networks for aspect-based sentiment analysis. In *Proceedings of the 59th Annual Meeting of the Association for Computational Linguistics and the 11th International Joint Conference on Natural Language Processing (Volume 1: Long Papers)*, pages 6319–6329.

Yanran Li, Hui Su, Xiaoyu Shen, Wenjie Li, Ziqiang Cao, and Shuzi Niu. 2017. Dailydialog: A manually labelled multi-turn dialogue dataset. *arXiv preprint arXiv:1710.03957*.

Sebastian Lindskog and Juan A Serur. 2020. Reddit sentiment analysis. *Available at SSRN 3887779*.

Dehong Ma, Sujian Li, Fangzhao Wu, Xing Xie, and Houfeng Wang. 2019. Exploring sequence-to-sequence learning in aspect term extraction. In *Proceedings of the 57th Annual Meeting of the Association for Computational Linguistics*, pages 3538–3547.

Andrew Maas, Raymond E Daly, Peter T Pham, Dan Huang, Andrew Y Ng, and Christopher Potts. 2011. Learning word vectors for sentiment analysis. In *Proceedings of the 49th annual meeting of the association for computational linguistics: Human language technologies*, pages 142–150.

Henry B Mann and Donald R Whitney. 1947. On a test of whether one of two random variables is stochastically larger than the other. *The annals of mathematical statistics*, pages 50–60.

Mainack Mondal, Leandro Araújo Silva, and Fabrício Benevenuto. 2017. A measurement study of hate speech in social media. In *Proceedings of the 28th acm conference on hypertext and social media*, pages 85–94.

Mahmoud Nabil, Mohamed Aly, and Amir Atiya. 2015. Astd: Arabic sentiment tweets dataset. In *Proceedings of the 2015 conference on empirical methods in natural language processing*, pages 2515–2519.

Ossama Obeid, Nasser Zalmout, Salam Khalifa, Dima Taji, Mai Oudah, Bashar Alhafni, Go Inoue, Fadhl Eryani, Alexander Erdmann, and Nizar Habash. 2020. Camel tools: An open source python toolkit for arabic natural language processing. In *Proceedings of the 12th language resources and evaluation conference*, pages 7022–7032.

Maria Pontiki, Dimitrios Galanis, Haris Papageorgiou, Ion Androutsopoulos, Suresh Manandhar, Mohammad Al-Smadi, Mahmoud Al-Ayyoub, Yanyan Zhao, Bing Qin, Orphée De Clercq, et al. 2016. Semeval-2016 task 5: Aspect based sentiment analysis. In *International workshop on semantic evaluation*, pages 19–30.

Hugo Rosa, Nádia Pereira, Ricardo Ribeiro, Paula Costa Ferreira, Joao Paulo Carvalho, Sofia Oliveira, Luísa Coheur, Paula Paulino, AM Veiga Simão, and Isabel Trancoso. 2019. Automatic cyberbullying detection: A systematic review. *Computers in Human Behavior*, 93:333–345.

Sara Rosenthal, Noura Farra, and Preslav Nakov. 2017a. Semeval-2017 task 4: Sentiment analysis in twitter. In *Proceedings of the 11th international workshop on semantic evaluation (SemEval-2017)*, pages 502–518.

Sara Rosenthal, Noura Farra, and Preslav Nakov. 2017b. SemEval-2017 task 4: Sentiment analysis in Twitter. In *Proceedings of the 11th International Workshop on Semantic Evaluation (SemEval-2017)*, pages 502–518, Vancouver, Canada. Association for Computational Linguistics.

Mohammad Salameh Saif M. Mohammad and Svetlana Kiritchenko. 2016. Sentiment lexicons for arabic social media. In *Proceedings of 10th edition of the the Language Resources and Evaluation Conference (LREC)*, Portorož, Slovenia.

Rodrigo Sandoval-Almazan and David Valle-Cruz. 2018. Facebook impact and sentiment analysis on political campaigns. In *Proceedings of the 19th Annual International Conference on Digital Government Research: Governance in the Data Age*, pages 1–7.

Richard Socher, Alex Perelygin, Jean Wu, Jason Chuang, Christopher D Manning, Andrew Y Ng, and Christopher Potts. 2013. Recursive deep models for semantic compositionality over a sentiment treebank. In *Proceedings of the 2013 conference on empirical methods in natural language processing*, pages 1631–1642.

Duyu Tang, Bing Qin, and Ting Liu. 2015. Learning semantic representations of users and products for document level sentiment classification. In *Proceedings of the 53rd Annual Meeting of the Association for Computational Linguistics and the 7th International Joint Conference on Natural Language Processing (Volume 1: Long Papers)*, pages 1014–1023, Beijing, China. Association for Computational Linguistics.

Zeerak Waseem and Dirk Hovy. 2016. Hateful symbols or hateful people? predictive features for hate speech detection on twitter. In *Proceedings of the NAACL student research workshop*, pages 88–93.

Charles Welch and Rada Mihalcea. 2016. Targeted sentiment to understand student comments. In *Proceedings of COLING 2016, the 26th International Conference on Computational Linguistics: Technical Papers*, pages 2471–2481, Osaka, Japan. The COLING 2016 Organizing Committee.

Elizabeth Whittaker and Robin M Kowalski. 2015. Cyberbullying via social media. *Journal of school violence*, 14(1):11–29.

Thomas Wolf, Julien Chaumond, Lysandre Debut, Victor Sanh, Clement Delangue, Anthony Moi, Pierric Cistac, Morgan Funtowicz, Joe Davison, Sam Shleifer, et al. 2020. Transformers: State-of-the-art natural language processing. In *Proceedings of the 2020 Conference on Empirical Methods in Natural Language Processing: System Demonstrations*, pages 38–45.

Mi Zhang and Tieyun Qian. 2020. Convolution over hierarchical syntactic and lexical graphs for aspect level sentiment analysis. In *Proceedings of the 2020 Conference on Empirical Methods in Natural Language Processing (EMNLP)*, pages 3540–3549.

Wenxuan Zhang, Xin Li, Yang Deng, Lidong Bing, and Wai Lam. 2021. Towards generative aspect-based sentiment analysis. In *Proceedings of the 59th Annual Meeting of the Association for Computational*

Linguistics and the 11th International Joint Conference on Natural Language Processing (Volume 2: Short Papers), pages 504–510.

Yazhou Zhang, Zhipeng Zhao, Panpan Wang, Xiang Li, Lu Rong, and Dawei Song. 2020. Scenariosa: a dyadic conversational database for interactive sentiment analysis. *IEEE Access*, 8:90652–90664.

Caleb Ziems, Bing He, Sandeep Soni, and Srijan Kumar. 2020. Racism is a virus: Anti-asian hate and counterhate in social media during the covid-19 crisis. *arXiv preprint arXiv:2005.12423*.

Eco EvE : Economic Event Extraction

Meriem Mkhinini, Mohamed Ali B.E.H Aissa, Aboubacar Sidiki Sidibe,
Paul Pike and **Aymen Khelifi**
Kaisens Data, 16 Pl. de l'Iris, 92400 Courbevoie
{mmkhinini, asidiki, ppike, aymen.khelifi}@kaisensdata.fr

Abstract

Every day, important events take place all over the world, but they are reported in various media outlets using various narrative tenses. Identifying real-world events have long been an important NLP problem. This paper, presents a comprehensive and up-to-date approach for economic events extraction in text-based context. We propose a zero-shot approach as an event extraction solution. The novelty of our approach rely in the use of separate glossaries to adapt to the domain application. It does require re-training to each specific type of events. The proposed approach, EcoEVE, is shown to be very effective when working with data from many platforms (Economic Calendar, Economic news...). Finally, we also present our ideas on future research directions.

1 Introduction

Event extraction is a challenging and long-researched task in information extraction (Grishman and Sundheim(1996)); (Riloff(1996)). The Automatic Content Extraction (ACE) program (ace()), defines an event as *something that happens. An Event can frequently be described as a change of state.* Based on the ACE program, we identify five main elements that form an event:

- **Event Type** : Thematic Event label describing the general nature of what's described in the sentence.
- **Trigger** : The word that most clearly expresses the event occurrence. In many cases, it is the main verb in the part of the sentence describing the event.
- **Agent** : The doer or instigator of the action denoted by the predicate.

Figure 1: An example of an event with extracted arguments.

- **Patient** : The undergoer of the action or event denoted by the predicate.
- **Time** : When the Event takes place
- **Place** : Where the Event takes place

Some event elements, such as the place or time maybe absent. However, an event my still occur. We give an example in Figure 1, which represents a 'Bankruptcy' event (the event type), triggered by "began" (the event trigger) and accompanied by its extracted arguments - text spans denoting entities that fulfill a set of (semantic) roles associated with the event type (e.g. `AGENT of the event, PATIENT or recipient of the event and TIME of the event`).

In this paper, we study event extraction based on context information, namely economical context. We address the following research question : Can context information improve the accuracy of event identification?

To address this question, we propose a three step model based on zero-shot classification. The later is a technique that allows the association of an appropriate label to a text. This association is irrespective of the text domain and the aspect.

In Section 2, we give a review of existing work. In section 3, we present the details of our proposed approach. In section 4, we present the data used to implement our model. Section 5, gives the results

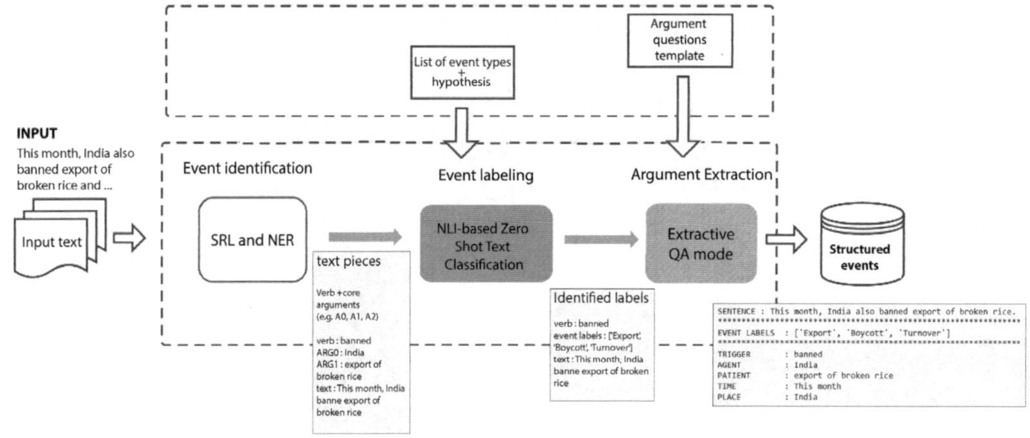

Figure 2: Our pipeline for event extraction.

obtained in our experiments. Finally, in section 6, we conclude the state of our work and present the future improvements.

2 Related Work

Recent successful approaches to event extraction usually require supervision (e.g., (Lin et al.(2020)Lin, Ji, Huang, and Wu)). Particularly, methods relying on expert systems, to define rules based on the occurrence of events in text. Such approaches can be labor-intensive and ignore the semantic meaning of event type labels.Economic events, however, can be formulated in many ways depending on specific domain they report (Arendarenko and Kakkonen(2012)).defining a domain ontology and rules for every application can be time consuming and difficult. Furthermore, defining a set of strict rules often results in low recall scores, since these rules usually cover only a portion of the many various ways in which certain information can be worded.

Zero-shot learning (ZSL) most often refers to a fairly specific type of task: learning a classifier on one set of labels, and then evaluating it on another set of labels that the classifier has never seen before. It has been used much more broadly to make a model do something for which it has not been explicitly trained. Evaluate a language model on downstream tasks (Radford et al.(2019)Radford, Wu, Child, Luan, Amodei, and Sutskever) without refining it directly on those tasks. In their pioneering work on more general zero-shot models, (Yin et al.(2019)Yin, Hay, and Roth) propose to formulate text classification tasks as a textual entailment problem (Dagan et al.(2006)Dagan, Glickman, and Magnini). This correspondence allows for the use of a trained model on natural language inference (NLI) to be used as a zero-shot text classifier for a wide variety of unseen downstream tasks.

Recent work ((Liu et al.(2020)Liu, Chen, Liu, Bi, and Liu); (Du and Cardie(2020))) have emphasized the link between question answering (QA) and EA in supervised system development. Similarly, several efforts have explored unsupervised methods. Using similarity-based methods (Peng et al.(2016)Peng, Song, and Roth) attempted to extract event triggers with minimal supervision. (Huang et al.(2018)Huang, Ji, Cho, Dagan, Riedel, and Voss) and (Lai et al.(2020)Lai, Nguyen, and Dernoncourt) explored trigger and argument extraction in a slightly different setting: training on certain event types and testing on unseen event types. Recently, (Liu et al.(2020)Liu, Chen, Liu, Bi, and Liu) proposed a QA-based argument extraction method that does not handle triggers. To the extent of our knowledge no method has been proposed to extract both event triggers and arguments without any event extraction training data. In this paper, we investigate the possibility of a paradigm for the event extraction task - formulating it as a Zeroshot/question answering (QA) task (Zhang et al.(2021)Zhang, Wang, and Roth).

3 Methodology

We propose a three step based approach for event extraction as illustrated in Figure 2. The first step is event detection: Given input text, we apply Semantic role labeling (SRL) (Collobert and Weston(2008)) to understand the role of each word in a sentence. Then we use Named Entity Recognition(NER) (Schmitt et al.(2019)Schmitt, Kubler, Robert, Papadakis, and LeTraon), to identify key elements in text like names of people, places, monetary values,etc. Once the pre-processing step accomplished, we use zero-shot classification to detect potential events in the Event labeling step. The third and final step is argument extraction. We use a pre-trained QA models to extract specific arguments concerning the event. All pre-trained models we use are based on BERT and BART, including a Zero Shot, a bart-large (Lewis et al.(2019)Lewis, Liu, Goyal, Ghazvininejad, Mohamed, Levy, Stoyanov, and Zettlemoyer) model trained on the MultiNLI (MNLI) data-set (Williams et al.(2018)Williams, Nangia, and Bowman) , and extractive QA model (Lyu et al.(2021)Lyu, Zhang, Sulem, and Roth) trained on QAMR. We illustrate each step of our approach in details in the following sections.

3.1 Pipeline Overview

Our pipeline for event extraction relies on The Zero Shot model (green box in Figure 2). In the pre-processing stage, we segment the text into sentences and apply data cleaning techniques based on the Spacy Python library (Honnibal and Montani(2017)). Then, for each sentence, given a set of event types , it creates hypothesis template of "this example is ..." for each type to predict the type of the premise. If the inference is entailment, it means that the premise belongs to that type. Finally, the extractive QA model (orange box in Figure 2) takes as input a context and a Wh-question. For each sentence, it extract the event trigger and type. Thus iteratively identifying candidate event arguments (spans of text) in the input sentence.

3.2 Trigger Extraction

We formalize Trigger Extraction as a Zero Shot Classification task. To get potential event triggers from a sentence, we first perform semantic role labeling (SRL) (Gardner et al.(2017)Gardner, Grus, Neumann, Tafjord, Dasigi, Liu, Peters, Schmitz, and Zettlemoyer) as a pre-processing step. We use the BERT-based Verb SRL model. The sentence is then split into "text fragments", each containing its SRL predicate and its core arguments (A0, A1, A2, etc.). Then, we pass each text fragment as a premise to the zero-shot model as well as a list of event types. The model returns the list of event types sorted with scores (most likely to be linked to the text fragment) with the first being the highest entailment probability. Then, we pass the highest three labels combined with hypotheses of the form "this text is about ... " or "is related to ... " inspired by (Yin et al.(2019)Yin, Hay, and Roth). For every hypothesis, the model returns the probability that it is entailed by the premise. If the very best entailment probability throughout all occasion sorts surpasses a threshold, we output the corresponding SRL predicate as an event trigger of this type.

3.3 Argument Extraction

We formalize the task of Argument Extraction as a sequence of QA interactions with the pre-trained extractive QA model. Given an input sentence and the extracted trigger, we ask a set of questions, and retrieve the QA model's answers as argument predictions. We design two templates with annotation guideline based questions as shown in table 1.

We describe the agent as the noun phrase or pronoun that identifies the person or thing which initiates or performs an action in a sentence. The patient being the person or thing that receives an action in a sentence. Time and place are straightforward. The place (Locative in linguistics) is the specification of the place where the action or event denoted by the predicate is situated. The time or date in the other hand is the period when the action or event took place. Then, the cause being the reason why the action happens and the aim is the reason for doing the action. Finally the variation and old/new value being the values that changed or are talked about in the sentence.

For each question, the model returns the probability for the answer. If the highest probability across two question templates surpasses a threshold, we output the corresponding argument. Since many argument types in the event template do not occur in every sentence. For example in the sentence : `The imports of their struggling economy drastically outweigh the exports.`, there is only an AGENT and PATIENT argument.

4 Data Description

One of the main difficulties we faced building our model, is finding open source event data sets. In this section, we describe the EcoEVE economic event labels annotation dictionary. The goal of

Argument	Template(1)	Template(2)
AGENT	Who is responsible for the {trigger} ?	what is responsible for the {trigger} ?
PATIENT	who is {triggered} ?	what is {triggered} ?
TIME	when the {trigger} happen ?	in what time the {trigger} happen ?
PLACE	where the {trigger} happen ?	in what place the {trigger} happen ?
AIM	why the {trigger} happen ?	for what reason the {trigger} happen ?
OLD_VALUE	what is the old value before the {trigger} ?	from what value it have {triggered} ?
NEW_VALUE	what is the new value after the {trigger} ?	to what value it have {triggered} ?
VARIATION	what is the variation of the {trigger} ?	
CAUSE	how the {trigger} happen ?	what is cause of the {trigger} ?

Table 1: Arguments and corresponding questions from templates.

	title	event	sentence
0	Consumer Inflation Expectations	Inflation	Inflation expectations in Australia increased ...
1	Consumer Inflation Expectations	Inflation	The November inflation expectation figure, bas...
2	Consumer Inflation Expectations	Inflation	The report further noted that uncertainty abou...
3	Consumer Inflation Expectations	Inflation	Wage expectations continue to be weak, with be...
4	Unemployment Rate	Employment	The number of unemployed grew by 120 thousand ...

Figure 3: test data frame.

the EcoEVE labels is to enable unsupervised data-driven event extraction in economic news. To do so, we use a lexicon of English event labels. We scrapped articles from the news site The Financial Times, Wikipedia articles describing companies and major economic events, Economic calendars(containing indicators in real-time as economic events are announced and the immediate global market impact) and The Economist articles (Authoritative global news coverage of world politics, economics and business). In total, we collected over 500 news articles. Combined with Glossary of economics, containing 473 economic term and definition. We identified 70 event labels. These events and activities relate to specific instances of events mentioned in the articles. For example, in some economic calendars, events are divided into categories that describe the event like Interest Rate, Inflation, GDP Growth, Foreign Trade,etc.

5 Experimental Setup and Results

To evaluate our approach, we built the tool EcoEVE. Event extraction has two tasks: Trigger/argument identification and event labeling, with trigger/argument having three sub tasks (trigger identification, argument identification, and argument classification). We test each task separately.

5.1 Trigger/Argument Identification

To evaluate trigger and argument extraction, we use an existing Data Collection used by (Liu et al.(2019)Liu, Huang, and Zhang) including 574 news groups, 2433 news reports, 5830 sentences. This data set gives us the arguments and the trigger verb for each sentence. However, since the results of this dataset only take into account the root verb of a sentence, we made some adjustments to our model. Thus, for this part, we used the Spacy Linguistic Features model to only work with the ROOT verbs as the syntactic dependency, i.e. the relationship between tokens. Our approach gives us results of more than 80% of triggers and about 50% of arguments with semantically correct types were successfully mapped.

5.2 Event Labeling

For a lack of official open source test set, we collected data from Trading Economics [1]. The site provides accurate information for 196 countries, including historical data and forecasts for more than 20 million economic indicators, exchange rates,

[1] https://tradingeconomics.com/

stock indices, government bond yields and commodity prices. We suppose that the articles titles contain the main event discussed in the article text. Then, for each text, we segment it into sentences. We manually selected the sentences that relate to the event proposed by the title. Our final data frame contains 436 sentences. Figure 3 shows the first few rows of our data set, including titles, events, and sentences. We identified 18 event types manually.

We tested our approach without changing the original event type lexicon. In doing so, we obtain real results as we would on a potential unknown use case. Since our model can predict more than one event label for a sentence, we suppose that if one of them is the same as the manually identified event type, the event label is correct. The tool successfully mapped 89% of the event labels in our test set.

6 Conclusion and Perspective

In this paper, we present a novel approach for event extraction based on zero-shot and QA event extraction system. We study the performance of QA/zero-shot models on event extraction data sets and how these strategies affect the performance of our pipeline. Our approach have shown positive result and performance. However, we also identified several key challenges of the current approach. For instance, a more generic formulation in the event labeling stage can lead to better performance and flexibility. For future work, we are working on incorporating a broader context, a paragraph/document level context, into our methods to improve prediction accuracy. We could also further refine the QA/zero-shot models to improve their performance for the event extraction task.

References

ACE (Automatic Content Extraction) English Annotation Guidelines for Event.

Ernest Arendarenko and Tuomo Kakkonen. 2012. Ontology-based information and event extraction for business intelligence. In *AIMSA*.

Ronan Collobert and Jason Weston. 2008. A unified architecture for natural language processing: Deep neural networks with multitask learning. In *Proceedings of the 25th international conference on Machine learning*, pages 160–167.

Ido Dagan, Oren Glickman, and Bernardo Magnini. 2006. The pascal recognising textual entailment challenge. In *Machine Learning Challenges. Evaluating Predictive Uncertainty, Visual Object Classification, and Recognising Tectual Entailment*, pages 177–190, Berlin, Heidelberg. Springer Berlin Heidelberg.

Xinya Du and Claire Cardie. 2020. https://doi.org/10.18653/v1/2020.emnlp-main.49 Event extraction by answering (almost) natural questions. In *Proceedings of the 2020 Conference on Empirical Methods in Natural Language Processing (EMNLP)*, pages 671–683, Online. Association for Computational Linguistics.

Matt Gardner, Joel Grus, Mark Neumann, Oyvind Tafjord, Pradeep Dasigi, Nelson F. Liu, Matthew Peters, Michael Schmitz, and Luke S. Zettlemoyer. 2017. http://arxiv.org/abs/arXiv:1803.07640 Allennlp: A deep semantic natural language processing platform.

Ralph Grishman and Beth Sundheim. 1996. https://aclanthology.org/C96-1079 Message Understanding Conference- 6: A brief history. In *COLING 1996 Volume 1: The 16th International Conference on Computational Linguistics*.

Matthew Honnibal and Ines Montani. 2017. spaCy 2: Natural language understanding with Bloom embeddings, convolutional neural networks and incremental parsing. To appear.

Lifu Huang, Heng Ji, Kyunghyun Cho, Ido Dagan, Sebastian Riedel, and Clare Voss. 2018. https://doi.org/10.18653/v1/P18-1201 Zero-shot transfer learning for event extraction. In *Proceedings of the 56th Annual Meeting of the Association for Computational Linguistics (Volume 1: Long Papers)*, pages 2160–2170, Melbourne, Australia. Association for Computational Linguistics.

Viet Dac Lai, Thien Huu Nguyen, and Franck Dernoncourt. 2020. https://doi.org/10.18653/v1/2020.nuse-1.5 Extensively matching for few-shot learning event detection. In *Proceedings of the First Joint Workshop on Narrative Understanding, Storylines, and Events*, pages 38–45, Online. Association for Computational Linguistics.

Mike Lewis, Yinhan Liu, Naman Goyal, Marjan Ghazvininejad, Abdelrahman Mohamed, Omer Levy, Veselin Stoyanov, and Luke Zettlemoyer. 2019. http://arxiv.org/abs/1910.13461 BART: denoising sequence-to-sequence pre-training for natural language generation, translation, and comprehension. *CoRR*, abs/1910.13461.

Ying Lin, Heng Ji, Fei Huang, and Lingfei Wu. 2020. https://doi.org/10.18653/v1/2020.acl-main.713 A joint neural model for information extraction with global features. In *Proceedings of the 58th Annual Meeting of the Association for Computational Linguistics*, pages 7999–8009, Online. Association for Computational Linguistics.

Jian Liu, Yubo Chen, Kang Liu, Wei Bi, and Xiaojiang Liu. 2020. https://doi.org/10.18653/v1/2020.emnlp-main.128 Event extraction as machine reading comprehension. In *Proceedings of the 2020 Conference on Empirical Methods in Natural Language Processing (EMNLP)*, pages 1641–1651, Online. Association for Computational Linguistics.

Xiao Liu, Heyan Huang, and Yue Zhang. 2019. https://doi.org/10.18653/v1/P19-1276 Open domain event extraction using neural latent variable models. In *Proceedings of the 57th Annual Meeting of the Association for Computational Linguistics*, pages 2860–2871, Florence, Italy. Association for Computational Linguistics.

Qing Lyu, Hongming Zhang, Elior Sulem, and Dan Roth. 2021. https://doi.org/10.18653/v1/2021.acl-short.42 Zero-shot event extraction via transfer learning: Challenges and insights. In *Proceedings of the 59th Annual Meeting of the Association for Computational Linguistics and the 11th International Joint Conference on Natural Language Processing (Volume 2: Short Papers)*, pages 322–332, Online. Association for Computational Linguistics.

Haoruo Peng, Yangqiu Song, and Dan Roth. 2016. https://doi.org/10.18653/v1/D16-1038 Event detection and co-reference with minimal supervision. In *Proceedings of the 2016 Conference on Empirical Methods in Natural Language Processing*, pages 392–402, Austin, Texas. Association for Computational Linguistics.

Alec Radford, Jeff Wu, Rewon Child, David Luan, Dario Amodei, and Ilya Sutskever. 2019. Language models are unsupervised multitask learners.

Ellen Riloff. 1996. *Automatically generating extraction patterns from untagged text.* In Proceedings of the national conference on artificial intelligence.

Xavier Schmitt, Sylvain Kubler, Jérémy Robert, Mike Papadakis, and Yves LeTraon. 2019. A replicable comparison study of ner software: Stanfordnlp, nltk, opennlp, spacy, gate. In *2019 Sixth International Conference on Social Networks Analysis, Management and Security (SNAMS)*, pages 338–343. IEEE.

Adina Williams, Nikita Nangia, and Samuel Bowman. 2018. http://aclweb.org/anthology/N18-1101 A broad-coverage challenge corpus for sentence understanding through inference. In *Proceedings of the 2018 Conference of the North American Chapter of the Association for Computational Linguistics: Human Language Technologies, Volume 1 (Long Papers)*, pages 1112–1122. Association for Computational Linguistics.

Wenpeng Yin, Jamaal Hay, and Dan Roth. 2019. https://doi.org/10.18653/v1/D19-1404 Benchmarking zero-shot text classification: Datasets, evaluation and entailment approach. In *Proceedings of the 2019 Conference on Empirical Methods in Natural Language Processing and the 9th International Joint Conference on Natural Language Processing (EMNLP-IJCNLP)*, pages 3914–3923, Hong Kong, China. Association for Computational Linguistics.

Hongming Zhang, Haoyu Wang, and Dan Roth. 2021. https://doi.org/10.18653/v1/2021.findings-acl.114 Zero-shot Label-aware Event Trigger and Argument Classification. In *Findings of the Association for Computational Linguistics: ACL-IJCNLP 2021*, pages 1331–1340, Online. Association for Computational Linguistics.

An empirical Comparison of Arabic Named Entity Recognition Methods: Application to the ALP Corpus

Mohamed Lichouri
USTHB, Algiers, Algeria
mlichouri@usthb.dz

Abstract

This study compares the performance of some existing approaches to the problem of Arabic Named Entity Recognition. The approaches under consideration are based on Sequence Labelling and Multi-Label Classification methods. We will use the ALP corpus, a newly produced corpus with more than 58 tags, as our single corpus for comparison in order to ensure a fair comparison. In other words, we'll use a 58-way categorization procedure to figure out what each token's tags are. Despite just employing a portion of the ALP corpus—ALP2 (50%) and ALP3 (25%)—an average accuracy of more than 88% was achieved, which make the results highly encouraging.

1 Introduction

Named Entity Recognition (NER) focuses on the challenge of identifying specific linguistic categories that share semantic characteristics, such as organization names, where despite their outward variances, they all communicate the same meaning. Furthermore, they commonly emerge in environments that are similar. Similar rules apply to names of individuals, places, or dates. Sometimes people think that the NER problem has been resolved. We can say that well-trained systems score almost as high as human performance, at the very least. Neural networks, rules-based systems, and statistical models like CRFs and Maximum Entropy have all been used to close the efficiency gap with humans. Consequently, why bother with it? Because NER today has more to do with data than it does with algorithms (Frederic Giannetti, 2018). This is true for high resourced and low resource languages such as Arabic. This is why, in this paper, we will highlight the important work done on Arabic Named Entity Recognition. In overall there is so much progress for NER in other language like English, German and French, as opposed to the Arabic Language. The complexity of the Arabic language, peculiarities in the Arabic orthographic system, non-standardization of the written text, ambiguity, and lack of resources are the main reasons for the minimum number of research in NER.

Another constraint is the non conformity between the different tagging model, where some adopt the rule token from foreign languages and applied to Arabic, whereas other like Abed Alhakim Freihat opted to create a more thoroughly list of tags which can express the maximum number and variation of the Arabic language. This is why in this paper, we have considered the corpus created by Abed Alhakim Freihat as a test ground. So the novelty of this paper relate to:

- The first use of a mega corpus (ALP) (Freihat et al., 2018a,b) that contains more than 2 millions tagged word.
- The first ever conduction of a 58-way classification in Arabic (to our knowledge).
- Conducting a comparison study between some existing approaches using some well known tools for NER.

The rest of the paper will be organised as follow. An extensive and exhaustive list of work have been presented as a reference in the section 2. In section 3, we will present a description of the used dataset, followed by the different used approaches in section 4 as well as the gotten results in section 5. Whereas we will conclude our paper in section 6.

2 Related Work

The first work (to our knowledge) on Arabic Named Entity Recognition (ANER) was done by Benajiba et al. (Benajiba et al., 2007), where they first build an ANER system for Arabic texts based-on n-grams and maximum entropy which is applied to their own training and test corpora (ANERcorp) and gazetteers (ANERgazet). An overall accuracy of 55.23% was achieved by this first experiment, which was further improved by 19 point by the same authors in their second work (Benajiba and Rosso, 2008) by using additional information such as Part-Of-Speech tags and Base Phrase Chunks and changing the probabilistic model from Maximum Entropy to Conditional Random Fields. Another ANER system was built by Shaalan and Raza (Shaalan and Raza, 2009) using a rule-based approach. The process used by the authors is as follow: (a) recognizing the named entities by using a Whitelist which is representing a dictionary of names, and a grammar, in the form of regular expressions then (b) applying a filtration mechanism to revise the gotten results in (a) by using metadata and also a Blacklist or rejecter for case of ill-formed named entities and last (c) a disambiguation of identical or overlapping textual matches returned by different name entity extractors to get the correct choice. NERA has achieved an average accuracy of over 80% for the 10 used NEs tags. An improvement of the coverage of the mis-classified person, location and organization named entities types by 69.93 per cent, 57.09 per cent and 54.28 per cent, respectively was achieved by NERA 2.0 by the same authors (Oudah and Shaalan, 2017) by following an hybrid approach that integrates both rule-based and machine learning-based NER approaches. By incorporating cross-lingual features and knowledge bases from English using cross-lingual links, Darwish (Darwish, 2013) show that such features have a dramatic positive effect on recall where the effectiveness of cross-lingual features and resources on a standard dataset has permit the author to achieve a relative improvement of 4.1% over the best reported result in the literature. In recent year, we note the work done by Lample et al.(Lample et al., 2016) where they introduce two new neural architectures—one based on bidirectional LSTMs and conditional random fields, and the other that constructs and labels segments using a transition-based approach inspired by shift-reduce parsers. The authors consider also that character-based word representations learned from the supervised corpus and unsupervised word representations learned from unannotated corpora are considered as two sources of information about words in their model.An overall accuracy of over 78% was obtained in NER in four languages (English, Spanich, German and Ducth) without resorting to any language-specific knowledge or resources such as gazetteers. There is also the work of Lhioui et al.(Lhioui et al., 2017) where they used the NooJ platform based on linguistic rules to manage an experiments on the pilot Arabic Propbank data to finally achieve a score of 87%, which they proclaim that improves the current state of the art in Arabic NE recognition. Where-as Elbazi and Laachfoubi (El Bazi and Laachfoubi, 2017) have introduced a features based on Latent Dirichlet Allocation (LDA) to investigate and analyze three different approaches for utilizing LDA, Topical Prototypes approach and Topical Word Embeddings approach. The authors proclaim that their experiments show that each of the presented approaches improves the baseline features, among which the Word-Class LDA approach performs the best (over 73%). Moreover, the combination of these topic modeling approaches provides additive improvements, outperforming traditional word representations as Skip-gram word embeddings and Brown Clustering. The same authors (Bazi and Laachfoubi, 2018) have recently investigated whether word representations can also boost supervised NER in Arabic by using word representations as additional features in a Conditional Random Field (CRF) model and compare in the same time three neural word embedding algorithms (SKIP-gram, CBOW and GloVe) and six different approaches for integrating word representations into NER system where the Brown Clustering achieved the best performance among the six approaches by an accuracy of 67%.

Corpus	**ALP2** (50%)	**ALP3** (25%)	**ALP**
# tokens	1.04M	524.28k	2.27M
# unique tokens	84.13k	64k	148k
# labels	1.04M	524.28k	2.27M
# unique labels	54	50	58

Table 1: ALP corpus statistics

3 Dataset

In this work, we used the ALP corpus (Freihat et al., 2018a,b). The whole corpus had been tokenized and tagged in a semi-supervised way, where the authors started by labeling a 200 tokens and used it as training to predict the tags of another set of 200 tokens. The resulted tags have been verified manually by an expert which resulted in a 400 tokens as a training dataset. The authors have repeated this process until they created this ALP corpus, which contain more than 2 millions fully tagged tokens. For this work we have divided this corpus to two sets, ALP2 and ALP3 sets. In table 1, we provide some statistics on the used corpora.

In the table 3, we will present the labels frequency in the total corpus.

Label	Frequency	Example
O	2069010	الاسمنت
B-LOC	42972	الكعبة
I-ORG	31537	الفلكي
B-PER	28247	يوسف
B-ORG	20826	لجنة
I-PER	20109	الباشا
I-LOC	19964	المتحدة
C+B-LOC	13128	ودمشق
B-MONTH	6581	سبتمبر
P+B-LOC	4947	بفيينا
P+B-ORG	2851	للجزيرة
B-DAY	2267	الاثنين
I-EVENT	2173	اليمن
ALLAH	1875	الله
B-EVENT	1424	قمة
C+P+B-LOC	1315	وبالسودان
B-MISC	1298	إيرباص
C+B-PER	1220	وضياء
I-MONTH	1112	الأول
C+B-ORG	968	والاتحاد
P+B-PER	768	لمحمد
I-MISC	621	رختر
B-CLAN	434	الروهينغا
I-AWARD	206	سلطان
B-TIME	197	الساعة
I-CLAN	192	العربية
P+B-EVENT	151	لمهرجان
I-TIME	138	العاشرة
C+P+ALLAH	114	ولله

Table 2: ALP corpus labels frequency and examples -Part 1-

Label	Frequency	Example
B-AWARD	105	نوبل
P+ALLAH	104	لله
I-PROPH	104	محمد
C+B-MISC	91	وأندروميدا
C+B-CLAN	73	وآل
P+B-MISC	67	للمريخ
C+ALLAH	59	والله
C+B-MONTH	43	وجمادى
C+B-EVENT	38	وحرب
C+B-DAY	25	وخميس
ALLAH+VOC	20	اللهم
P+B-CLAN	15	لبني
C+P+B-PER	15	ولابن
C+B-AWARD	15	وجائزة
P+B-PROPH	10	للرسول
P+B-AWARD	8	لجائزة
C+P+B-ORG	2	وللأمم
B-CHAPTER	2	الفاتحة
C+P+B-PROPH	1	وللرسول
B-ORH	1	كيف
C+B-TIME	1	والثالثة

Table 3: ALP corpus labels frequency and examples -Part 2-

4 Approaches

We will present in this section our two proposed approach where the first one is our proposed approach which is based on Multi-Label Classification technique whereas the second is the Sequence Labeling approach.

4.1 Multi-Label Classification Approach

In this approach, we address the problem of NER as a simple Multi-Label Classification problem. Where the labels in the used corpus are considered as class candidate. For example if we have 5 label, the classification will be a 5-way classification approach. The following algorithm (–see algorithm 1)will summarize the different step for this approaches.

Algorithm 1 Multi-Label Classification

```
procedure MULTI-LABELCLASSIFICATION(corpus)
    Preparing Train and Test Data ▷ (Step 1)
    Convert Train and Test Data to array ▷ (Step 2)
    Applying TFidf transformation
    Training Phase for LSVM, BNB, MNB, LR, SGD and PAC ▷ (Step 3)
    for W ∈ Test do ▷ Testing Phase (Step 4)
        Predicting the Class of W by the six classifier
```

4.2 Sequence Labelling Approach

When the aim of NER is to extract the name of country, person in a text, we can note that the human being, when reading a news article he would usually recognise that a word or a phrase refers to a country, a person name, even when he has not seen that name before. The main reason is that there are many different cues in the sentence or the whole article that can be used to determine whether a word or a phrase is a country name or person name. This is where this approach perform well, because it take advantage of the surrounding context when labelling tokens in a sequence, where a commonly used method is the conditional random field (CRF). Which is a type of probabilistic graphical model that can be used to model sequential data, such as labels of words in a sentence.

In CRF, a set of feature functions, will be designed to extract features for each word in a sentence. During model training, CRF will try to determine the weights of different feature functions that will maximise the likelihood of the labels in the training data.

In the following algorithm 2, we will present the main steps for sequence labeling a word in a sentence.

Algorithm 2 Sequence Labeling

```
procedure SEQUENCE LABELING(corpus)
    Generating Part-of-Speech Tags ▷ (Step 1)
    for W ∈ corpus do ▷ Generating Word Features (Step 2)
        f1 := Convert W[i] to lower case
        f2 := Prefix/Suffix of W[i]
        f3 := W[i-1] (previous), W[i+1] (next)
        f4 := if(W[i]) is Uppercase or Lowercase (1 or 0)
        f5 := if(W[i]) is Number or Contains digit (1 or 0)
        f6 := PosTag(W[i]), PosTag(W[i-1]), PosTag(W[i+1])
        f7 := if(W[i]) contains special character (1 or 0)
    Split to train and test set ▷ (Step 3)
    Train CRF Model ▷ (Step 4)
    for W ∈ test do ▷ Testing phase (Step 5)
        Predict the tag of W[i] by CRF.tagger
```

5 NER Experiment Setup and Result

Because the ALP corpus has a huge number of instance, we couldn't conduct the desired experiments, this is why we decided to use only the half of the corpus, which give use slightly more than 1 Million labeled token, lets name it **ALP2**.

5.1 Multi-Label Classification Experiments

We considered a set machine learning techniques using the scikit-learn library (Pedregosa et al., 2011), namely: Support Vector Machines (SVM), Bernoulli Naive Bayes (BNB), Multinomial Naive Bayes (MNB), Logistic Regression (LR), Stochastic Gradient Descent (SGD) and Passive Aggressive (PAC). For this classifiers we opted for the default configuration as in the scikit-learn.

	Precision	Recall	F1-Score	Accuracy
LSVC	81%	87%	83%	86,73%
BNB	66%	81%	73%	81.27%
MNB	78%	84%	79%	84.40%
LogReg	79%	86%	81%	85.67%
SGD	76%	83%	76%	82.81%
PAC	80%	86%	83%	86.15%

Table 4: Detailed Results on a non shuffled dataset. Precision, Recall and F1-score are in average mode.

	Precision	Recall	F1-Score	Accuracy
LSVC	85%	90%	87%	90.38%
BNB	76%	86%	80%	86.45%
MNB	82%	88%	84%	88.46%
LogReg	84%	90%	86%	89.54%
SGD	82%	88%	83%	87.93%
PAC	84%	90%	87%	89.81%

Table 5: Detailed Results on a shuffled dataset. Precision, Recall and F1-score are in average mode.

For this approach, we carried-out two experiments: the first without shuffling the data (see table 4), when splitting the corpus to train and test.

Where-as the second by shuffling the data (see table 5). As mentioned earlier, we took only half of the ALP corpus, with a size of 1.04 Million tokens (ALP2). We divided this corpus to a 80% for train and the rest for test. For this approach, the best results has been gotten by the **LSVC** classifier when shuffling the data with an average accuracy of 90.38%.

	Setup	Accuracy
w/o Pos-Tags	ALP3	100%
	ALP2	99.9%
+ Pos-Tags	ALP3	90.1%
	ALP2	87.1%

Table 6: Accuracy gotten with sklearn-crf.

5.2 Sequence Labeling Classification Experiments

We used the code in [1] by Francois Vanderseypen. This tools is based on the sklearn_crfsuite[2],which permit to label a sequence of word with or without using Pos-Tags information. This is why we conducted four experiments: two with Pos-Tags and two without Pos-Tags using different setups. The gotten results as well as a description of the used dataset is described in table 6. We should note that we used for once 50% of the ALP (let's name it ALP2) and for the second 25% of ALP (let's name it ALP3). This choice was made because of the lack of computing power.

If we consider the same setup as for the first Approach, while using the ALP2 corpus, the best results achieved by this approach is with a an accuracy of 99.9% without using the Pos-Tags. Whereas, while using the ALP3 corpus, a perfect accuracy was obtained without using Pos-Tags. If we consider the Pos-Tags information, we noted a decrease of about 10% in accuracy.

6 Conclusion

We presented in this paper an empirical comparison between two approaches and two tools. Where the first approach is based on a Multi-Label Classification Methods and the second approach is based on a sequence labeling methods (two tools). For the Multi-Label Classification, the best results was achieved by LSVM with an accuracy of 90.38%, which is very encouraging because the time of training is very low in comparison to the other tool. Or the tool, which is based on sklearn-crf has achieved some excellent results, despite the very long training time.

[1]https://github.com/Orbifold/dutch-ner

[2]https://github.com/TeamHG-Memex/sklearn-crfsuite

References

Frederic Giannetti. 2018. Named Entity Recognition: Challenges and Solutions. `https://blog.doculayer.com/named-entity-recognition-challenges\-and-solutions`. Online; accessed 18 December 2022.

Ismail El Bazi and Nabil Laachfoubi. 2018. Arabic named entity recognition using word representations. *arXiv preprint arXiv:1804.05630.*

Yassine Benajiba and Paolo Rosso. 2008. Arabic named entity recognition using conditional random fields. In *Proc. of Workshop on HLT & NLP within the Arabic World, LREC*, volume 8, pages 143–153. Citeseer.

Yassine Benajiba, Paolo Rosso, and José Miguel Benedíruiz. 2007. Anersys: An arabic named entity recognition system based on maximum entropy. In *International Conference on Intelligent Text Processing and Computational Linguistics*, pages 143–153. Springer.

Kareem Darwish. 2013. Named entity recognition using cross-lingual resources: Arabic as an example. In *Proceedings of the 51st Annual Meeting of the Association for Computational Linguistics (Volume 1: Long Papers)*, pages 1558–1567.

Ismail El Bazi and Nabil Laachfoubi. 2017. Arabic named entity recognition using topic modeling. *context*, 230.

Abed Alhakim Freihat, Mourad Abbas, Gábor Bella, and Fausto Giunchiglia. 2018a. Towards an optimal solution to lemmatization in arabic. In *Fourth International Conference On Arabic Computational Linguistics, ACLING 2018, November 17-19, 2018, Dubai, United Arab Emirates*, volume 142 of *Procedia Computer Science*, pages 132–140. Elsevier.

Abed Alhakim Freihat, Gabor Bella, Hamdy Mubarak, and Fausto Giunchiglia. 2018b. A single-model approach for arabic segmentation, pos tagging, and named entity recognition. In *2018 2nd International Conference on Natural Language and Speech Processing (ICNLSP)*, pages 1–8. IEEE.

Guillaume Lample, Miguel Ballesteros, Sandeep Subramanian, Kazuya Kawakami, and Chris Dyer. 2016. Neural architectures for named entity recognition. *arXiv preprint arXiv:1603.01360.*

Chahira Lhioui, Anis Zouaghi, and Mounir Zrigui. 2017. A rule-based approach for arabic temporal expression extraction. In *2017 International Conference on Engineering & MIS (ICEMIS)*, pages 1–6. IEEE.

Mai Oudah and Khaled Shaalan. 2017. Nera 2.0: Improving coverage and performance of rule-based named entity recognition for arabic. *Natural Language Engineering*, 23(3):441–472.

Fabian Pedregosa, Gaël Varoquaux, Alexandre Gramfort, Vincent Michel, Bertrand Thirion, Olivier Grisel, Mathieu Blondel, Peter Prettenhofer, Ron Weiss, Vincent Dubourg, et al. 2011. Scikit-learn: Machine learning in python. *the Journal of machine Learning research*, 12:2825–2830.

Khaled Shaalan and Hafsa Raza. 2009. Nera: Named entity recognition for arabic. *Journal of the American Society for Information Science and Technology*, 60(8):1652–1663.

ALRT: Cutting Edge Tool for Automatic Generation of Arabic Lexical Recognition Tests

Osama Hamed
Computer Systems Engineering Department
Palestine Technical University
Tulkarm - Palestine
osama.hamed@ptuk.edu.ps

Saeed Salah
Department of Computer Science
Al-Quds University
Abu Dis, Jerusalem, 20002, Palestine
sasalah@staff.alquds.edu

Abed Alhakim Freihat
Department of Computer Science
University of Trento
Trento - Italy
abed.freihat@unitn.it

Abstract

A Lexical Recognition Tests (LRT) is a common tool being widely used to measure the level of language-learner's proficiency utilizing vocabulary size (or simply the number of words acquired by a learner) for several international languages like English, Arabic, German, Chinese, and Spanish. Compared to other languages, LRT themes for Arabic are not mature enough and still they have some rooms for improvement, with very few existing proposals that mainly use human-crafted or semi-automated methods using Arabic Natural Language Processing (NLP) techniques. This paper introduces ALRT, the Arabic Lexical Recognition Tests Tool for the automatic generation of Arabic LRTs. The tool was tested using a huge dataset of Arabic vocabulary, and a subject-matter expert intervention was involved as an extra validation step to verify the quality of generated nonwords.

1 Introduction

Arabic is one of the main languages being widely used. It is not only spoken by more than 422 million people, but also non Arab people are using Arabic to practice Islam, study Arab cultures, and collect Arabs' opinions about many topics, etc. (Abdelgadir and Ramana, 2017). Arabic is mainly divided into three classes; standard, spoken and classical (Elfardy and Diab, 2012). The standard Arabic is the language used for official documents, language learning centers, and educational resources and books; the spoken Arabic constitutes the main spoken language of Arabs in modern society, it has many dialects that represent various diversities of the real spoken Arabic language - Levant, Moroccan, Gulf, Levant, and Egyptian- which leads to to so-called Arabic "Diglossia", i.e., Arab people use the same word/phrase to express different meanings; and the classical Arabic is the language of the ancient people, the Holy Quran and Arabic classical books were written using this language.

Some research contributions to Arabic natural language processing argued that Arabic lacks efficient approaches to measure Arabic learning proficiency using simple, fast, and efficient placement tests. Arabic Lexical Recognition Tests (ALRT), modules, applications and tools are still under development stages, (Salah et al., 2022); (Hamed, 2019), (Hamed and Zesch, 2018). According to (Hamed and Zesch, 2017), the Lexical Recognition Test (LRT) is a vocabulary size test, which is frequently used to calculate the number of words known by or acquired by a language learner. In such a test, the language learner is shown a list of vocabularies, and for each vocabulary, he/she needs to determine whether it is a valid word or nonword, and the LRT scores can be easily measured based on the learner's responses. Figure 1 shows a sample item of this test for both English and German. The main advantages of the LRT are it is simple, fast, and efficient. A test examiner roughly needs several minutes to answer all questions. LRTs come in two formats: a set of Yes/No questions or a customized checklist format.

Like English and German, as the number of Arabic learners increase, the necessity to have such kind of Arabic placement tests (LRT) increases as well. Currently, Arabic learning centers lack such kind of effective approaches to measure learners proficiency level. Thus, this research is a further step of our more recent work aiming at developing an Arabic LRTs tool, called ALRT (Arabic Lexical Recognition Tool. In the work (Hamed, 2019; Salah et al., 2022), we proposed a generic framework for the automatic generation of Arabic LRT, and developed an algorithm that follows some rules to generate high-quality nonwords that can confuse language learners and add certain levels of complexity, thus they are good distractors. Furthermore, this method applies some paradigms based on (i) statistical machine learning such as character n-gram models, and (ii) Arabic language special

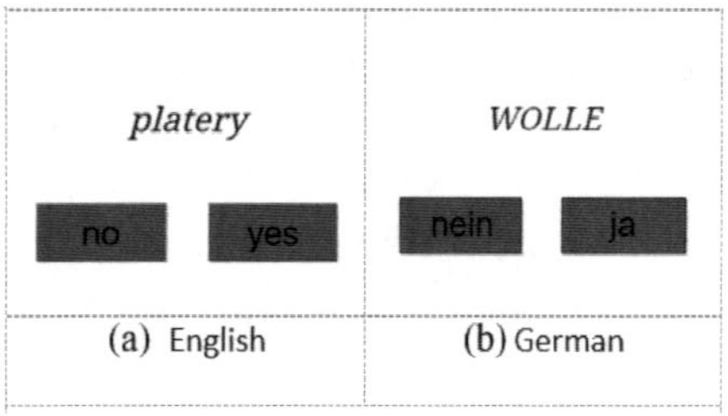

Figure 1: Examples of Yes/No questions

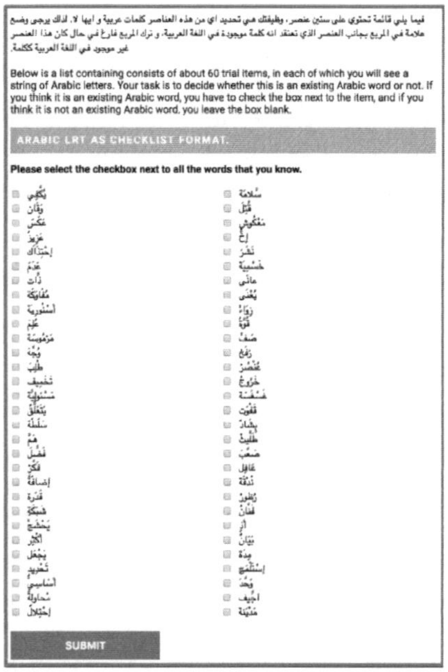

Figure 2: An example of Arabic LRT (ALRT)

characteristics such as orthography and phonological similarity maps. Finally, we applied some additional language features using word frequency map to generate multiple levels of Arabic LRT. Its worth noting that the adopted approach is mainly based on similar approaches that were applied on some European languages such as Spanish and German. Figure 2 shows a sample output of ALRT.

The remaining parts of the paper are structured as follows. The most relevant contributions are discussed in Section 2. Section 3 discusses some potential applications of using the ALRT tool. The current state of the tool is presented in Section 4. Finally, Section 5 concludes the paper and provides some ongoing research lines.

2 Related Work

Recently, measuring language proficiency levels has been attractive for many researchers. The lexical project (Balota et al., 2007) is one of the main contributions in this field, it is the common criterion being widely used to measure learning proficiency levels, it contains many international standard tests for any specific language. For example, the International English Language Testing System (ILETS), and the Test of English as a Foreign Language (TOEFL). Both tests are adopted by English-native countries to measure English language proficiency levels for official use such as business, work, academic, and international mobility, among others. The Lexical Recognition test (LRT) is another example, which is a short and quick test that is frequently used to estimate learners' proficiency for some international languages such as English, German, Spanish, and other Latin languages. Many related experiments, research, and contributions coming from various European centers have approved this concept with the help of real test beds and datasets. In the following, we shed light to the most relevant contributions for Arabic and discuss their main drawbacks. Consequently, we avoid the potential issues related to similar experiments that were conducted to design this form of tests previously. Also, we avoid some literature review associated with Arabic diacritics during the process of generating good nonwords like (Hamed and Zesch, 2017).

LexTALE is another criterion used to test language proficiency for English and German languages (Lemhöfer and Broersma, 2012). LexTALE is a five-minute, YES and NO vocabulary identification test. In its default settings, it consists of 60 questions, two-thirds are words and one-third are nonwords. Its performance shows good results when applied on a processed dataset of vocabularies. However, compared to other tests like the Test of English for International Communication (TOEIC), it is still substantial.

In Arabic, nonwords were manually generated by language experts who follow certain rules to generate high quality nonwords. This process is inefficient, time consuming and sometimes subjects to human errors. As the quality of nonwords plays a crucial role in determining accurate scores, high quality nonwords must be very similar both phonologically and orthographically to real words to increase the complexity of identifying them easily. LexTALE is a valid test that was adapted by other languages like German, French, and Spanish, and it can be used as a good measurement criterion for non-native language speakers who have various learning levels - small, medium, and high. (Duyck et al., 2004).

Generating the nonwords manually was also applied by English Lexicon Project (ELP) (Balota et al., 2007). It is a huge repository of language resources and databases both descriptive and behavioral, connected with a search engine that supplies the researchers with all resources they need to tackle any technical issue and obstacle they face during the process of implementing the lexical tests. Technically, the ELP is totally built using manual procedures to generate nonwords. This process is done by applying certain roles and language characteristics to replace one or more characters in a word with others to create a nonword with high similarity index to the original one considering orthographic and phonological characteristics. A similar work was applied to the British-English language (Rastle et al., 2002). The ARC nonword database was used by applying a generation model based on both phonological and orthographic rules. This ARC database was used to design the LRT test that tricks the learner in multiple ways based on the morphological, orthographic, and phonological rules.

The Wuggy research project (Keuleers and Brysbaert, 2010) developed a computer-based application that facilitates the process of generating nonwords automatically, it creates high quality pseudo words or nonwords following certain rules of languages, features, sub-syllabic structure, and transition frequencies among sub-syllabic elements. It is available for many languages such as English, Spanish, French, German, Basque, and Serbian. It could be applied to other languages with some extra efforts. In this regard, a pseudo word is given a more attention and can be taken as another important factor for determining the efficiency of the lexical decision, which represents a good tool by psycholinguists who perform word processing tasks. The Wuggy algorithm has some limitations (i) its dependency on sub-syllabic or summed bi-gram similarities decreases its performance; (ii) it is not a fully automated solution for nonword generation, it requires some human intervention to write the matching expressions; (iii) the algorithm has some technical issues in auto detecting the end of the given expression.

WordGen is another application which is similar to Wuggy, it is an automated tool used to generate and select nonwords for English, French, and German (Duyck et al., 2004). Here, both automatic and manual methods have been collaboratively used to generate nonwords. Other researchers (Hamed and Zesch, 2015), (Hegazi, 2016) argued on the importance of the role of Arabic diacritized in vocabulary assessments in the LRT, as they claimed that diacritization adds a new level of complexity and reveals ambiguity that introduces better evaluation for learners in identifying the words. Consequently, a sample test using both the diacritized version of Arabic LRT and the non-diacritized version was generated to show the importance of Arabic diacritization compared to other languages. The results showed that the absence of Arabic diacritization increases the ambiguity of word recognition. It is worth noting that the majority of Arabic written text is non diacritized, except in some religious, historical, classical books, and in some specialized Arabic educational fields. Diacritization impacts the design of nonwords as Arabic diacritization is an orthographic way to describe Arabic word pronunciation (Hamed and Zesch, 2017). They assumed that the non-diacritized nonwords are highly probably more difficult to guess than the diacritized ones. The diacritized nonwords can easily distract the language's learners when having more closely related words, especially if they come with labels having pronounceable diacritics.

In (Hamed and Zesch, 2015), Hamed and Zesch suggested the use of a fully automated methodology to generate high-quality nonwords for English LRTs. To implement the automated process of generating nonwords in English, they conducted some experiments to generate good nonwords using some methods based like Markov and character language models that automatically replace a letter with similar one. They also applied some mechanisms to rank the generated nonwords and used the highest ones in creating English LRT.

Similarly, in (Rastle et al., 2002), the authors developed an automatic paragdimg to generate nonwords for English Language. They constructed a database of nonwords based on both phonetic and orthographic language properties.

3 Applications of ALRT

The authors in (Gueddah and Yousfi, 2013) proposed an approach to improve Arabic spell checking in typing text. They suggested the use of a statistical model based on a similarity matrix to find Arabic letters' similarity degrees, this way each

Table 1. Summary of the raw dataset (dimensions and references).

Corpus Source	File Name	Char Count	Lines	Size [KB]	Diacritized
Al-Jazeera Corpus[1]	aljazeera.txt	13,260,976	80,369	13,058	No
Al-Jazeera Corpus[1]	aljazeera100.txt	977,321	5,887	955	No
Books Corpus[2]	books.txt	858,622	1,533	839	No
KACST Corpus[3]	KACST.TXT	24,551,235	74,106	23,976	No
KACST Corpus[3]	KACST100.txt	1,077,781	74,106	1,053	No
Al-Khaleej-2004 Corpus[4]	khaleej.txt	27,283,987	5,695	26,645	No
Al-Khaleej-2004 Corpus[4]	Khaleej100.txt	1,106,419	231	1,081	No
Al-Watan-2004 Corpus[4]	Wata100.txt	1,043,107	178	1,019	No
Al-Watan-2004 Corpus[4]	Watan.txt	124,202,282	178	121,292	No
Watan Diac Corpus[4]	Watan-diac.txt	163,473,924	40,579	159,643	Yes
Quran[5]	quran.txt	743,918	6,236	727	No
RDI[6]	rdi.txt	858,844	2,579	839	No
Tweets[7]	Tweets-ann.txt	1,528,273	10,007	1,493	No
Tweets[7]	Tweets-sharp.txt	1,514,713	10,007	1,480	No
WikiNews[8]	WikiNewsTruth.txt	177,279	423	174	No
Total		**362,658,681**	**312,114**	**354,274**	

1 URL: http://www.aljazeera.net/portal [Online; Last Accessed 29th, July, 2020].
2 URL: https://sourceforge.net/projects/tashkeela/ [Online; Last Accessed 29th, July, 2020].
3 URL: https://sourceforge.net/projects/kacst-acptool/files/ [Online; Last Accessed 29th, July, 2020].
4 URL: https://sites.google.com/site/mouradabbas9/corpora [Online; Last Accessed 29th, July, 2020].
5 URL: http://tanzil.net/download/ [Online; Last Accessed 29th, July, 2020].
6 URL: http://www.rdi-eg.com/RDI/TrainingData/ [Online; Last Accessed 29th, July, 2020].
7 URL: https://www.aclweb.org/anthology/D15-1299 [Online; Last Accessed 29th, July, 2020].
8 URL: https://www.aclweb.org/anthology/W17-1302 [Online; Last Accessed 29th, July, 2020].

Arabic letter has a matrix of weighted degrees of similarities with other Arabic letters by assigning costs to the permutation errors generated by using the proximity degrees of keyboard characters and the calligraphic similarity in Arabic alphabet. Their aim was to develop a spell checking tool for malformed words that are created during the writing of Arabic documents. In a comparison to this work, we found another similarity matrix for each Arabic letter based on Arabic orthographic and phonological characteristics, so reputations will be performed based on a small set of similarities. Although the two works have different scopes, the main objective is to have an Arabic LRT that can be used as Arabic spellchecker. Compared to previous research contributions, this research work develops ALRT tool which is based on a proposed approach that considers generating the nonwords in a fully automated process using a newly developed algorithmic that implements some Arabic language characteristics such as spelling, orthography, pronunciation, phonology, n-grams, and the word frequency map which is mainly used to create multiple complexity levels of LRT test. In this regard, it wroth noting that to generate nonwords, we have been inspired by their definition: "words that fulfill the phonological constraints of the language but do not bear the meaning" (Huibregtse et al., 2002).

Another approach to generate nonwords in English is using minimal pairs (Ricks, 2015), a corresponding way to implement this concept in Arabic is the use of orthography and phonology roles. (Hamed and Zesch, 2015) argued that frequent n-grams are highly likely to generate high quality nonwords, which look like real words, and words that appear more frequently are easier to remember than less frequent words (Ellis, 2002). In addition to that some generated nonwords in Arabic could be classified as fake Arabic vocabulary that look like real words that were designed to distract the learners and confuse them in terms of phonetic if they tried a pronunciation or an orthographic letter that differ in terms of word writing shape.

In summary, to get a better picture of the practical value of the developed tool, we shed the light on three potential applications: First, since LRT themes are common methods to measure language learners' proficiency levels. However, the existing LRTs research for Arabic still has room for improvement, with few existing proposals at development stages, or existing proposals that mainly use human-crafted methods, or semi-automated methods using Arabic NLP techniques. Thus, an interesting application of the developed tool is to measure the proficiency level of Arabic learners (Arabic LRT). Fig. 3 shows an example of Arabic LRT that fits on one page. Second, another potential application is the Arabic spellchecker. Since the proposed approach can potentially generate a huge amount of good nonwords, these nonwords can be incorporated into any Arabic Proofreading tool that can be used as a reference model for spell-checking documents written in the Arabic for checking consistency, accuracy, and readability to meet professional standards. Third, since Arabic LRTs are still in the development stages, the proposed approach can be used as a reference by Arabic language researchers, who want to conduct relevant studies. The source code, the implementation steps, the documentation, and the generated nonwords database will be freely available on the GitHub platform. For now, we have uploaded the LRT test engine (https://github.com/ohamed/ar-lrts).

4 Current State of the Tool

The current version of the ALRT is V1.0, it is the initial draft that was built based on our previous work ((Salah et al., 2022)). Recently, we have proposed a generic framework for the automatic generation of Arabic LRT, and developed an algorithm that follows certain rules, and features to generate high quality nonwords with high similarity index to the original ones, and introduces certain levels of complexity to the LRT. In this work, we used a freely available corpora datasets that were collected from different resources, such as Arabic books, social media, and news agencies. It has a huge volume of Arabic texts in raw format that were transformed to one UTF-8 format having one vocabulary per line. Some preprocessing steps were also applied to make the data format suitable to work with. In data preprocessing, we mainly applied some data cleaning operations to remove special symbols, non Arabic characters, punctuation marks, numeric values, white-spaces, and any other strange character. Table 1 lists some technical features about the dataset. Column (1) represents the main corpus source; the available source of the data, some sources might have multiple files (rows in the table), number of alphabets, lines as in a notepad++ text file, size in Kilobytes (KB), whether the text is diacritized or not diacritized, and the main reference. Figure 3 shows the proposed block diagram of Arabic Lexical Recognition Test (LRT) ((Salah et al., 2022)), which is the tool we developed to generate Arabic nonwords.

Algorithm 1: The proposed algorithm for nonwords generation

```
start procedure
Initialize: NonwordList()=null, ProcDSList,
SimilarityList= null, Frequency, Threshold1,  Threshold2
// First step: Read random word from ProcDSList
  loop      // For each word in ProcDSList
   word = getNewWord()
    Frequency = ProcDSList.count(word)
    if (Threshold1 < Frequency < Threshold2) {
      LO = ListofOrthographics(word)
       LP = ListofPhonologics(word)
       SimilarityList= LP+LO
   endif
   Nonword =getRandomWord(SimilarityList)
   if (ProcDSList.find(Nonword) == False)
        NonwordList.add(Nonword)
   else
        SimilarityList.del(Nonword)
        goto step (11)
end procedure
```

4.1 Nonwords generation - Orthographic and phonological

The process of automatic generation of Arabic nonwords is based on the common Arabic language features, such as orthographic, phonological, n-grams, and vocabulary frequency. Algorithm 1 describes the pseudo-code for generating the nonwords. The proposed algorithm beings by iterating through all processed vocabularies found in the database. For each vocabulary, the algorithm calculates its frequency. To generate multilevel LRTs, the algorithm computes the word's frequency (how many times the chosen word appeared in the corpus). To tune the algorithm's operation in terms of words' frequencies, we used two thresholds - Threshold1 and Threshold2. If Frequency > Threshold1 && Frequency < Threshold2, we assume that the given vocabulary is not used more frequently. Two lists will be created, one contains the orthographic vocabularies using orthographic similarity roles, and the other contains phonological vocabularies using phonological similarity map. next, the two list are merged to construct the similarity list that includes all vocabularies. The algorithm randomly selects a set of vocabularies from the similarity list "SimilarityList" and checks the occurrence of them in the processed data. If the selected vocabulary is a real word, it will be removed from the similarity list. The algorithm repeats the process to select a new vocabulary.

4.2 N-grams generation

To further improve the automatic generation of nonwords, the results of Algorithm 1 have been updated by implementing the character n-grams concepts that represent the subsequent characters of vocabulary. This process iterates through the processed data file, and then for each vocabulary, it generates all possible n-grams starting from bigram to word-length-1 grams. These n-grams were appended to the database table along side with their corresponding real words, this step is useful in formulating a statistical data reference for which conclusions and judgements can be built easily. Since n-grams could be involved in generating nonwords by replacing a character in the input word taking into consideration frequency occurrence of prefix and postfix characters. Consequently, the closet character from the similarity set intersected with a character that uses frequency in the n-grams list will be substituted. This way, n-grams are being used to narrow the acceptable possibilities; this is expected to improve the quality of the nonwords generation process.

5 Conclusion and Future Work

In this paper, we have introduced the Arabic Lexical Recognition Tests Tool (ALRT) for the automatic generation of Arabic LRTs. The proposed tool will automatically generate nonwords based on a newly proposed model, which considers Arabic special characteristics such as orthography (spelling), phonology (pronunciation), n-grams, and the word frequency map, which is an important factor to create a multi-level test. The tool was tested using a huge dataset of Arabic vocabulary, and a human-driven intervention was used as an extra verification step to validate the quality of generated nonwords. We are working on integrating the ALP (Freihat et al., 2018b,a) lemmatizer for generating lemmas automatically. We also plan to add other Tests to the tool such as tokenization recognition tests, part of speech recognition, and diacritization recognition tests.

References

Ehsan Mohammed Abdelgadir and VSV Laxmi Ramana. 2017. *A Handbook on "Introduction to Phonetics & Phonology": For Arabic students*. Notion Press.

David A Balota, Melvin J Yap, Keith A Hutchison, Michael J Cortese, Brett Kessler, Bjorn Loftis, James H Neely, Douglas L Nelson, Greg B Simpson, and Rebecca Treiman. 2007. The english lexicon project. *Behavior research methods*, 39(3):445–459.

Wouter Duyck, Timothy Desmet, Lieven PC Verbeke, and Marc Brysbaert. 2004. Wordgen: A tool for word selection and nonword generation in dutch, english, german, and french. *Behavior Research Methods, Instruments, & Computers*, 36(3):488–499.

Heba Elfardy and Mona Diab. 2012. Aida: Automatic identification and glossing of dialectal arabic. In *Proceedings of the 16th eamt conference (project papers)*, pages 83–83.

Nick C Ellis. 2002. Frequency effects in language processing: A review with implications for theories of implicit and explicit language acquisition. *Studies in second language acquisition*, 24(2):143–188.

A. A. Freihat, M. Abbas, G. Bella, and F. Giunchiglia. 2018a. Towards an optimal solution to lemmatization in arabic. In *Proceedins of the 4th International Conference on Arabic Computational Linguistics (ACLing 2018)*, pages 1–9.

A. A. Freihat, G. Bella, H. Mubarak, and F. Giunchiglia. 2018b. A single-model approach for arabic segmentation, pos tagging, and named entity recognition. In *2018 2nd International Conference on Natural Language and Speech Processing (ICNLSP)*, pages 1–8.

Hicham Gueddah and Abdallah Yousfi. 2013. The impact of arabic inter-character proximity and similarity on spell-checking. In *2013 8th International Conference on Intelligent Systems: Theories and Applications (SITA)*, pages 1–4. IEEE.

Osama Hamed and Torsten Zesch. 2015. Generating nonwords for vocabulary proficiency testing. In *Proceeding of the 7th Language and Technology Conference: Human Language Technologies as a Challenge for Computer Science and Linguistics*, pages 473–477.

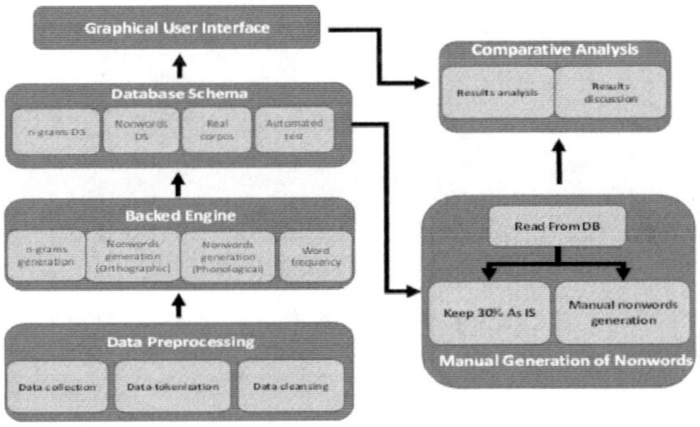

Figure 3: The proposed block diagram of Arabic Lexical Recognition Test (LRT)

Osama Hamed and Torsten Zesch. 2017. The role of diacritics in designing lexical recognition tests for arabic. *Procedia Computer Science*, 117:119–128.

Osama Hamed and Torsten Zesch. 2018. The role of diacritics in adapting the difficulty of arabic lexical recognition tests. *NLP for Computer Assisted Language Learning (NLP4CALL 2018)*, 23.

Osama Amin Hamed. 2019. *Automatic generation of lexical recognition tests using natural language processing*. Ph.D. thesis, Dissertation, Duisburg, Essen, Universität Duisburg-Essen, 2019.

Mohamed Osman Hegazi. 2016. An approach for arabic root generating and lexicon development. *Int. J. Comp. Sci. Netw. Sec.(IJCSNS)*, 16(1):9.

Ineke Huibregtse, Wilfried Admiraal, and Paul Meara. 2002. Scores on a yes-no vocabulary test: Correction for guessing and response style. *Language testing*, 19(3):227–245.

Emmanuel Keuleers and Marc Brysbaert. 2010. Wuggy: A multilingual pseudoword generator. *Behavior research methods*, 42(3):627–633.

Kristin Lemhöfer and Mirjam Broersma. 2012. Introducing lextale: A quick and valid lexical test for advanced learners of english. *Behavior research methods*, 44(2):325–343.

Kathleen Rastle, Jonathan Harrington, and Max Coltheart. 2002. 358,534 nonwords: The arc nonword database. *The Quarterly Journal of Experimental Psychology Section A*, 55(4):1339–1362.

Robert Stephen Ricks. 2015. *The development of frequency-based assessments of vocabulary breadth and depth for L2 Arabic*. Georgetown University.

Saeed Salah, Mohammad Nassar, Raid Zaghal, and Osama Hamed. 2022. Towards the automatic generation of arabic lexical recognition tests using orthographic and phonological similarity maps. *Journal of King Saud University-Computer and Information Sciences*, 34(10):8429–8439.